good News preaching

GOODNEWS PREACHING

Offering the Gospel in Every Sermon

GENNIFER BENJAMIN BROOKS

Foreword by Ronald J. Allen

THE PILGRIM PRESS
CLEVELAND

The Pilgrim Press, 700 Prospect Avenue, Cleveland, Ohio 44115-1100
thepilgrimpress.com

Scripture quotations, unless otherwise noted, are from the New Revised
Standard Version of the Bible, © 1989 by the Division of Christian Education of
the National Council of Churches of Christ in the United States of America and
are used by permission. Changes have been made for inclusivity.

Printed in the United States of America on acid-free paper

14   13   12   11   5   4   3

Library of Congress Cataloging-in-Publication Data

Brooks, Gennifer Benjamin, 1947–
    Good news preaching : offering the Gospel in every sermon /
Gennifer Benjamin Brooks ; foreword by Ronald J. Allen.
        p. cm.
    Includes bibliographical references (p.   ) and index.
    ISBN 978-0-8298-1822-2
    1. Preaching.   2. Bible—Homiletical use.   I. Title.
BV4211.3.B755 2009
251—dc22   2008051414

CONTENTS

CONTENTS

Living into the Promises

foreword

Imagine stepping into the pulpit on Sunday morning or Saturday night and looking into the faces of the congregation. What do you see? An older woman whose husband was interred last month and who is in the grip of grief. A young couple trying to conceive a child. A woman sitting at a strange angle on the pew because her husband hit her again. Three people in their late fifties who work at the local plant whose supervisors told them on Friday that the plant will close in three weeks. A high school student struggling with feelings of attraction toward persons of the same gender. Parents who have a child serving in Iraq for whom every news bulletin is a moment of panic. A lesbian couple who have just been told that their application for adoption has been refused—again. A member is resentful because you did not get to the hospital quickly enough while that person was there. A secret drinker. One member who has been convicted of a crime and is awaiting sentencing and another who was surprised at home late at night by an intruder in the bedroom. And this first impression of the congregation does not take into account the full range of the news that comes across the television, internet, radio, and newspaper, from violence and poverty and racial/ethnic tensions to environmental catastrophe in so many corners of the world.

What do such folk need to hear from your sermon?

Before passing too quickly to the answer to that question, here is one more. What are the deepest yearnings of *your* own heart? Love? Peace? Grace? Hope? A feeling that you can make a difference? A sense that you and the congregation are indeed a *community* of witnesses?

What do you, the preacher, need to receive from the Bible, from Christian doctrine, and from the heart of the gospel itself?

People in all of these circumstances—and many others—share a common need: *to hear good news from God.* They need to know that God is present for them and what God is doing on their behalf and on behalf of the whole world. They need to be empowered to respond to the divine love, and to know how to do so.

Some listeners need to feel God's immediate care and providence for them. Some must repent from personal sin and move toward restoring relationships. Some need to turn away from complicity with injustice and become agents of systemic change. As a preacher, I often approach the pulpit with shaking hands, dry mouth, and lingering questions. I need to be reminded that the Holy Spirit can move through me like electricity through a cable.

In this transforming book, Professor Gennifer Brooks articulates an exquisite biblical and theological rationale for why good news should be the basic character of Christian preaching. She offers practical guidance in how to identify good news in biblical passages and how to correlate that news with life situations today. These backgrounds point to the climax of the volume: how to shape sermons that give voice to the good news in both content and form.

Some readers are undoubtedly tapping their fingers on the desk and thinking, "But what about sin? What about condemnation and prophetic challenge?" Be assured. This book does not reduce the good news to positive thinking. Still less is it a gospel of success or a handbook for a happy middle- or upper-class life. Professor Brooks grew up in the Caribbean but spent her adult life in New York City, where she has been an eyewitness to exploitation, racism, sexism, and violence. She knows the struggle that Christian life can be. This book is no pablum, but rather looks these fierce realities in the eye, and yet it is bold enough to assert that when reality has done its worst, the good news from God is still at work. No matter how bitter or battered any situation, it is not beyond the reach of God's regenerating presence, and that is good news.

In this regard, Gennifer Brooks stands on the deepest biblical and theological foundations. The Hebrew language often employs the word *basar* and its cognates to speak of good news. For example, in Psalm 68:11 the good news (NRSV: "tidings") is that the enemies of Israel flee as Israel enters the promised land. Psalm 96:2 exults that the good news (NRSV: "tell") is God's salvation, God's reign, which means the possibility of justice and right relationships (Ps. 96:10, 13).

In the Torah, Prophets, and Writings, the language of good news reaches its most powerful expression in Isaiah 40–55. The leaders of Israel are in exile. They are discouraged and without hope. To them the prophet says, "Get you up to a high mountain, O Zion, herald of good tidings [good news], lift up your voice with strength, . . . lift it up, do not fear; say to the cities of Judah, 'Here is your God!'" The good news is not only that God is present but that God is at work to release them from exile, to return them home, and to do it all like a shepherd gathering the lambs in his arms (Isa. 40:9–11; cf. 41:27).

Indeed, in an evocative passage that continues to define the calling of the preacher, Isaiah declares, "How beautiful upon the mountains are the feet of the messenger who announces peace, who brings good news, who announces salvation, who says to Zion, 'Your God reigns'" (Isa. 52:7; similarly 60:6; 61:1). The good news is that God, like a monarch, triumphs over the enemies of the welfare of the community.

The Septuagint—the translation of the Hebrew scriptures into Greek and the version of the Gospels, Torah, and Writings that was used by early followers of Jesus—uses the word *euangelion* to speak of the good news. This word is made up of the prefix *eu*, meaning "good" and the noun *angelos*, meaning "news." By definition, then, the gospel is news that has a good quality.

For the apostle Paul the notion of *euangelion* is so important that he uses it to describe both apostolic vocation and the heart of the apostolic message. Paul is "set apart for the gospel of God" (Rom. 1:1). The gospel is "the power of God for salvation" (Rom. 1:16–17). For Paul, the good news is that through Jesus Christ, God is ending the present evil age and is leading the world towards an apocalypse (the second coming of Jesus), after which God will remake the cosmos as the divine realm in which all things will take place according to God's purposes. Indeed, when Paul outlines the motives for his own ministry in Romans 10:15, he draws upon Isaiah 52:7.

The first three gospels describe and assert the leading theme of the ministry of Jesus in this way. The first words of Jesus in the Gospel of Mark interpret his entire ministry. "The time is fulfilled, and the realm [NRSV: kingdom] of God has come near; repent and believe in the good news [*euangelion*]" (Mark 1:15). The good news is that God has set in motion the movement towards the eschatological world. Jesus is God's agent in that movement. Matthew uses very much the same language (Matt. 4:17). Luke introduces the ministry of Jesus with Jesus' sermon in the synagogue at Nazareth in which Jesus quotes from the great Isaiah to explain the Savior's vocation. "The Spirit of [God] is upon me, because [the Spirit] has anointed me to bring good news to the poor " (Luke 4:18; Isa. 61:1).

Without turning this foreword into an exercise with the concordance, we can see these themes throughout the Gospels and Letters. We find good news as the guiding message in Paul's epistles (for example, Col. 1:5; Eph. 3:8; 1 Tim. 1:1; 2 Tim. 1:8). The most fully preserved early Christian sermon, the Letter to the Hebrews, understands the fundamental message to be that of good news (Heb. 4:2), as do Peter's (1 Pet. 1:12) and the pinnacle of the Bible (Rev. 14:6).

In all of these biblical authors, the good news of God is *good* precisely because the bad news of the world is so bad. Whether people understand themselves as befouled by the stain of sin, or suffering undeserved tragedy, or imprisoned by unjust systems, or as the victims of missed possibilities, Christian tradition asserts that God is present not only to comfort their hurts but also to transform their circumstances. The distance from the ambiguous present to God's overflowing future may be long and hard, but it is a journey taken in hope because it is a journey towards transformation and regeneration that is beyond our imagining and deeper than our desiring. I know of no better guide on that journey than Professor Gennifer Brooks.

Ronald J. Allen
Nettie Sweeney and Hugh Th. Miller
Professor of Preaching and New Testament,
Christian Theological Seminary

pReface

"Now ain't that good news!"

My greatest desire when I listen to sermons is to be able to say these words when the preacher sits down. Sadly, that has not been my response to many of the sermons I've heard over the past few decades. My desire to do something about the situation has been the impetus behind this book. It has taken two years to come to fruition, and along the way I have listened to many persons who sit in church pews and have lamented with them the need for real good news from our preachers. Writing this book has been a joyful and challenging experience. Throughout, I have tried to follow the leading of the Holy Spirit and the whispers of God.

Preaching is the proclamation of the gospel to the people of God in a particular time and place. The word "gospel," translated from a Greek word (*euangelion*), meaning good news, implies that the act of preaching is intended to offer good news to the hearers of the preached word. The good news that preaching has to offer even in this post-modern world is the always new thing that God is doing in the redemption of the world through Jesus Christ. Samuel Proctor believes "preaching helps us to find answers to the mystery of human suffering and misfortune,"[1] and that in and of itself is good news. However in my experience of listening to sermons over the past few decades, there is too often little, if any, good news offered to the people. Sometimes the good news that is offered is shallow and lacks theological depth, and too often it does not relate in a significant and concrete way to the everyday lives of the congregation.

From the outset let me state clearly that I am not suggesting that sermons should be all sweetness and light; nor am I advocating the dreaded prosperity gospel that so many in the church find objectionable. To the contrary, I am a strong advocate of presenting a realistic picture of human sinfulness as always being in need of the redemptive grace of God; but my deep theological conviction is that such presentation should be done only if there is an even stronger offering of divine grace. As was brought home to me recently in the response to a sermon I preached, if the good news makes living in challenging times seem too easy, it loses authenticity. Nor is it appropriate to simply offer a sinecure for real issues of life by directing the hearers to turn to Jesus. The good news that the sermon offers must be realistic from the standpoint of human possibility even as it rests securely on God's unstinting grace.

Thus as I thought about what would be the focus of my first book on preaching, I was struck by the need for real sermonic good news. I was influenced also by the challenge such a requirement presents to many of my students and their difficulty or downright inability to discern authentic good news from the biblical text and to offer that good news in their sermons. And as I listened more closely to preachers, even many who are often commended publicly for their preaching, I was struck by how many gave short shrift to offering good news in the construction and delivery of their sermons.

Recently, while discussing the focus of this writing with a preacher in training, I was challenged with the question: "Does every sermon need to have explicit good news?" This budding preacher tried to convince me that good news was implied in all sermons because behind the proclaimed word was always the good news of Jesus' redemption of humanity that is the basic tenet of Christianity. That same preacher also claimed that there were some sermons in which it was impossible to give good news, perhaps because of a particular biblical text or the context in which the sermon was preached.

Of course I disagreed, as I believe that the sermon offers a definitive and always opportune place for the proclamation of the grace of God. Good news must be proclaimed clearly because its purpose is to help shape the people of God in their Christian discipleship, and the sermon is the primary vehicle by which the preacher names the good news of God's ongoing act of deliverance. The sermon is a medium by which the preacher offers testimony and bears witness to the unending presence of the grace of God in scripture, in the world, and in the individual and corporate lives of preacher and congregation. As Ron Allen states it, "The sermon is good news not only because it helps the congregation perceive that God is repairing the destructive work of sin, but also because God is constantly in the world to manifest love, justice and other forms of blessing."[2] Thus the good news of the sermon cannot offer simply a feel-good response to the bad news of human sin; it must reveal God's grace present in the application of the good news to the substance of their lives.

My experience as a discerning listener of sermons began in my troublesome teen years. My pastor, the Reverend William W. Watty, a leading theologian of Caribbean origin, preached "good" sermons. I could not have told you then what made them good, but on reflection I believe that it was because, first, they did not make me feel chastised even though I was aware of places within myself and actions that I was doing that were less than what was expected of me as an active member of the church. But more than that, they affirmed me as a child of God, one who continued to experience God's love in the midst of evidence that named me, in my mind, as unworthy. And long before I became an elder in the United Methodist Church and accepted my calling as a minister of the Word of God, I was convicted about the need to offer some semblance of good news to hurting people whenever I preached.

Listening to the feedback from congregations I have been privileged to serve solidified in me the belief that as much as the people of God need to confront and admit to their sinfulness, to seek God's justifying grace, and to be challenged to live out their discipleship faithfully, they just as urgently need to hear that they are not alone in their struggles, that God's grace is already theirs and ever available to support their Christian endeavors. As a result, it became a critical element in my preaching that at all times my sermons offered hearers explicitly the good news of God's active, empowering, transforming presence that alone could enable them to fulfill their commitment as disciples of Jesus Christ. My pastoral experiences convinced me that people are hungry for the good news of God's presence with them as they strive to live faithfully as Christians; and those same experiences convicted me as to the necessity for every preached sermon to offer recognizable good news.

As a teacher of preaching, it is difficult not to listen to sermons in a regular congregation on a Sunday morning with a critical ear, so I strive intentionally to take off my "professor head" when I attend worship services. What that means is that I refuse to allow myself to evaluate the sermon for form and structure, but I listen intentionally for good news. I do so because I need it as much as every Christian does. In a world that has seemingly gone mad in so many ways, each sermon must be a reminder or, better said, an affirmation, that whatever the trouble we face individually, in society, or in the world, God is still present and active, not only redeeming the world, but also enabling us to live beyond the challenges of our everyday world through that redemptive, transforming, empowering grace. Indeed, the preacher must understand that sermons not only need to name and claim the good news, but also that without that good news the sermon cannot be effective in meeting its purpose of proclaiming the gospel.

This is what good news preaching offers. It is intentional in framing the sermon around good news that represents the transformative, regenerative action of God. Good news preaching speaks to the divine/human relationship in which God is doing something in us that engages our participation, so that in effect we are prepared for and even impelled into a life of discipleship in Jesus Christ. The good news sermon offers an alternative to lulling words that deny the reality of human sin and to demanding rhetoric that lays additional burdens on the already mission-minded Christian. Good news preaching offers the covenantal grace of God that meets and responds to the reality of human sin and need.

In the chapters that constitute the substance of this text, I will frame the requirements for developing and preaching sermons that are intentional in offering good news. Chapter 1 lays claim to the essential nature of the sermon as good news, and to the importance of recognizing the good news from God as the beginning point of sermon development. Chapter 2 deals with the foundational nature of scripture as the source of both the sermon and the good news and interpretive models to bring the good news of the text to light. Chapter 3 focuses on the theological nature of the sermon and the necessity of appropriate theological understanding in the ongoing conversations between God, the preacher, and the people. Chapter 4 looks at the contextualization of the sermon for preaching through the juxtaposition of text and context. Chapter 5 offers practical models for developing sermons of different styles in an attempt to help preachers identify and select sermonic styles that are suited to both the scripture text that is the foundation of the sermon, and the delivery of good news for the particular context. Chapter 6 moves the sermon from the study to the pulpit and focuses on the preacher's role in giving testimony through engaging delivery of the sermon and particularly through the effective presentation of good news. A brief concluding word is followed by four good news sermons of varying styles.

There are many persons who have walked with me through the journey to bring this work to fruition. To each I say thank you and pray God's blessings on your life. However I must name a few special persons. Words seem inadequate to thank Ron Allen, in many ways my writing partner, who volunteered to read my writing in its most primitive form. His direction guided my musings and helped to sharpen my prose. I am also grateful for the kind words of his foreword to the book.

Heartfelt thanks go to Bishop Edsel A. Ammons, who expressed his hopes for the book on behalf of the church he loves so much and then read and threw his support behind the manuscript. Thanks also to the members of the Word in Worship seminar at the 2008 meeting of the North American Academy of Liturgy—Craig Satterlee, Brian

Hartley, Amy Schifrin, and Paul Galbreath—who read and responded with affirmation and support to the material presented to them. Special thanks go to my preaching classes at Garrett-Evangelical Theological Seminary, many of which became the laboratory for testing the appropriateness and clarity of what I wrote.

And then there are the people who help to make my life's journey more complete: my sisters, Pearl, Akua, and Yvette; my brothers, Michael and Sele; my nieces, Marcia and Charmaine; my nephews, Robert and Chaka; and my grandniece and nephew, Nyah and RaSean; my prayer partner, Iris Green; my clergy confidant, Leo Curry; my closest friend, Janet Telemaque, and Shirley Parris, without whose typing skills the task would be close to impossible. Then there are those special friends and colleagues who step up or show up when they are called—and even when they are not but think they are needed: Gerlyn Adams, Helen Ammons, Antoinette Anthony, Valerie Bridgeman-Davis, Indra Dorman, Hortence Drew, Jacqueline Ford, Norma Grant, Gertrude Hunte, Gayle Isles, June Johnson, Ouida Lee, Bob Martindale, Cynella Simon, Ernest Swiggett, Anthony Toole, Linda Tyson, Dorothy Watson-Tatem, David Welch, Eastlyn Welch, and Sylvia Young.

My grateful appreciation to my community at Garrett-Evangelical Theological Seminary, who support me in ways too numerous to mention, and women within that community—like Cheryl Anderson, Diane Bogues-Hill, and Pamela Lightsey, who offer companionship for the journey. There are many other persons, unnamed but greatly appreciated, who support my work in many ways. For all of them I give thanks and praise to God.

Finally, and above all, thank you, Holy Spirit, for your empowering wisdom.

My prayer for this text is that some preacher, new or experienced, may find in its thesis and its contents a new vision for his or her task as preacher of the Word of God and may join in witness to the omnipresent grace of God through sermons that offer genuine good news to the people of God.

oNe

■

The Sermon *Is* Good News

t was the third Sunday of Advent and the title of the sermon printed in the worship bulletin was "The Meaning of Christmas." Although I knew that there were Advent messages worthy of preaching based on the lectionary scripture texts, I was not troubled by the preacher's focus on Christmas and I looked forward to hearing this important gospel message revealed once again. What I heard for the fifteen minutes that this preacher spoke was a history lesson on the origin of the celebration of Christmas Day—in essence, how December 25 became a Christian holiday. I was in turn stunned, disconcerted, bewildered, and finally angry. I tuned out the service as my brain went into overdrive imagining the many ways that this preacher could have helped the congregation focus on the real meaning of Christmas. Perhaps second only to his resurrection, I believe the birth of Jesus the Christ offers the most obvious good news of Christianity: how could any preacher fail to present the truly good news of Christmas to the congregation? Observing the many blank faces in the sanctuary, I wondered what this preacher had been taught about and understood as the purpose of preaching.

Preaching is above all the proclamation of the gospel: the good news of Jesus Christ as Savior of the world. What I mean by good news being essential to the sermon is the subject of this chapter. I discuss the sources of good news, the importance of explicitly presenting good news, and the work of the Holy Spirit in making the good news of the sermon effective in our lives. I also look at the nature of the sermon as good news in the context of worship.

A DEFINITION OF THE SERMON AS GOOD NEWS

"What is preaching?" This question is the beginning point of any class I teach or any workshop I lead on the subject of preaching. The answers in all cases are almost as many and as varied as the number of people in attendance. From my own reflection and from the many responses to that essential question, I have developed a short list of definitions that speak to the critical nature of preaching as good news. Preaching is:

- The proclamation of the gospel to the people of God in a particular time and place.
- Interpretation of the gospel to bring alive its relevance to the congregation for the shaping of their individual and communal lives.
- Helping people experience the assurance of grace that is the gospel of Jesus Christ.
- Offering the gathered community an opportunity to celebrate and claim the love of God in Jesus Christ.
- Providing guidance for interpreting and responding ethically to personal and social issues of life through the gospel.

This is by no means an exhaustive list, nor does it fully represent the various definitions offered in response to my question or that I have read over the years. What these definitions have in common is that they name as an ingredient in the sermonic construction the gospel or good news of God's grace.

Other definitions offered by my students were not so explicit but alluded to the expectation that the preacher would say something that would help people to become good or better disciples of Jesus Christ. Some respondents believed that it was the task and the responsibility of the preacher to remind the hearers of their sinfulness and to call them to live according to the example of Christ. When pressed to suggest how such hearers could be helped, the respondents could seldom provide a useful solution.

That gap always helped to move the discussion to a second question: the purpose of preaching. Respondents generally agreed that preaching was about delivering the Word of God, and the preacher was identified as prophet, the mouthpiece of God, who had the responsibility of delivering a message from God. In the course of ensuing conversations, respondents admitted that often the definition and the reality of preaching (as proclamation of good news) were at odds with one another. They reluctantly admitted that often more time is spent on assuring hearers of the divine inspiration of the preacher's message than on emphasizing its good news. Expanding on the notion of divine origin, some students felt that while the message would vary depending on the circumstance, it should respond to the needs of the people, whatever the preacher considered them to be. And since the preacher had received the message from God, its God-directed contents did not have to be explicitly good news. That God would choose to interact with people in part through the preacher's message was good news in itself.

In fact, in response to a third question on the nature of the sermon, the general response was that the sermon was a message from God. Seldom did students offer the idea that the words of the sermon were required to be recognizable as good news. Even those who named the gospel in their definition of preaching and who expressed their understanding of the good news as human redemption through Christ most often did not connect it directly with the need to make that good news explicit in every sermon. There was common acceptance that God's grace, active and present in human life, was good, but most expected that this was generally understood by congregations and did not need to be stated explicitly each time one preached. The purpose of the sermon, they believed, was essentially to call hearers to recognize their sin and encourage or command them to follow the teachings of Christ in order to ensure their salvation. As such, the criterion of good news was achieved by the very existence of the sermon, a message from God, which was evidence of God's presence in and interaction with the community.

I agree with students and other preachers that the sermon must be a word from God. However, as a message from God, each sermon provides the opportunity to make explicit the good news of God's redemptive, sanctifying grace that continues to be an active force in human endeavors and specifically for living as Christians. To fit its definition as good news the sermon must make relevant to the present congregation this interaction between God and human beings. In doing so, the message of the sermon establishes its authenticity as the Word of God, essential to hearers for living as the people of God. As Marjorie Suchocki states it, "our very lives depend upon our being hearers of God's Word."[1] As human beings and Christians, we are always in the process of becoming like Christ, such that, in the language of the Wesleyan tradition, the hope for our eternal salvation is that we are going on to perfection,[2] and the reality is that we cannot attain that state of being without the grace of God. The sermon can be an effective medium for presenting the good news of God's sustaining grace, and the preacher is charged to recognize and take advantage of this opportunity in every moment of preaching.

So for a long time I resisted using the terms "the good news sermon" or "good news preaching" because I believe that every sermon is about proclaiming good news. That changed as I became convinced that one ought intentionally to develop and name the good news of each sermon. Since the purpose of the sermon is to enable hearers to experience the proclamation of good news, each sermon must presumably offer good news. In scripture, prophetic messages of God's anger toward God's chosen people are always mediated by words of hope and grace. Again and again the prophets are charged by God to offer a mitigating word to people who incurred the wrath of God because of their failure to keep the covenant. The Christian preacher likewise is charged with offering the same word of God that speaks of God's willingness and readiness to offer grace to bring about the transformation necessary for faithful Christian living. Recognition of this legacy is the beginning point for developing a sermon as good news.

The content of the sermon is good news when it offers evidence of the presence and grace of God active in scripture, in the life of the church, and in individual lives. But it is not simply restating history that makes this true. The sermon is good news only when its voice moves beyond echoes of the past; when the word of scripture is instructive and enlivening; when the message of God's love is recognized as timeless and delivered as active and available; and when the grace of God is offered freely to all in the present as text meets context in the lives of the hearers. Although the concept of news implies and most often refers to the reporting of past events, the good news sermon as God's message is not simply anchored in past events. It is descriptive and representative of present reality and future promise of divine-human interaction that is based on the substance of God's eternal, covenantal love for humanity revealed in scripture. Thus the presence of explicit good news is an important element in every sermon and in every act of preaching as it enlivens, awakens, and energizes preacher and people for joyful living even in a troubled world.

THE IMPORTANCE OF NAMING GOOD NEWS IN THE SERMON

The purpose of preaching is to bring the Word of God and specifically to offer the good news of God's love for and continued relationship with humanity. The sermon as the medium by which the preacher presents the divine word must be a proclamation of this good news. Hearing a definition of preaching as good news for the first time in a seminary preaching class jolted me, and the impact of the words sped through my system as forcefully as shock waves emanating from a disturbance in the cosmos. For a few moments I withdrew mentally from the class. My memory of the sermons over the years that failed totally to meet this definition is what jolted me. I remembered the fire and brimstone sermons from visiting evangelists during my childhood years; the sermons that exhorted the hearers to admit their evil ways and give up such soul-destroying actions as dancing and drinking and called hearers to come forward in confession and repentance of their sin; the messages that encouraged listeners to give of their money, time, and talents; even the sermons that urged acceptance of Jesus Christ through baptism. And as my memory playback continued, only once in a while did any of these remembered sermons seem like good news in any way.

The grace of God that the professor claimed was the substance of the gospel message was either unrecognizable or absent from the sermons that flooded my mind. I was led to wonder about the interpretation of the preaching task and the content of the sermon that seemed to be the norm for Christian preachers. In fact I questioned whether it was the seminary professor that was in error given the widespread lack of good news in sermons preached over the centuries of Christianity. Some of the same questions that emerged that day also floated through my mind on the Advent Sunday noted previously, and fortunately on both occasions I was able eventually to locate several sermons that fit the criteria of proclaiming good news. I found that among the great number of sermons that had formed me, there were those that stood out because of the affirming word they offered. And as I delved into those memories, their theme of God's free offering of redeeming love seemed to grow in importance and helped to solidify my conviction that every sermon needed to speak of the reality of God's grace that alone enables us to live faithfully as Christians. In those good news sermons of pleasant memory the preacher had clearly presented the grace of God as active in the lives of every individual present, in their personal situations, and in the world at large, enabling those who claimed it to live fully as children of God.

We need good news in sermons because of our sinfulness. Sin causes brokenness to both individuals and communities and is experienced not only through the physical pain and suffering of sickness and disease, but also through moral and spiritual infirmities such as injustice and oppression. Systemic ills of society feed untenable situations of poverty and hunger, unemployment and homelessness, addiction and disease, and all manner of situations that also contribute to abuse and oppression of individuals and groups. The problems of violence and the evils of injustice are widespread and serve as stark reminders of the active presence of sin in the world. The preacher has the responsibility to name these ills since there can be no true repentance until one admits to the reality of individual and corporate sin in the world. As prophet, the preacher of the Word of God must call people to acknowledge their sinfulness, since confrontation with sin is the starting point of the way of salvation and is meant to lead the people to the act of repentance. But even at this early stage, the preacher has good news to share, good news that arises from the covenantal relationship between God and human beings, and that the preacher must offer to the listening congregation.

John Wesley named the initial act of divine love as preventing (or prevenient) grace,[3] because it prevents people from giving in to their basest human desires. Yet, we need more. So the preacher calls hearers to seek the forgiving grace of God also, for it is this forgiving grace that enables them to live according to the example of Christ and achieve holiness of heart and life. The authenticity of the sermon lies first in its ability to juxtapose divine love with human sin, and then to engage the hearts of the hearers to believe in and depend upon that love as powerful and effective against the temptations and ungodly desires that confront their hearts and minds. Divine grace as the enabling power of Christian living is the unfailing good news that each sermon can present. Members of the congregation are confronted with life challenges that they can meet or overcome only through the grace of God. The preacher brings a message of God's grace available to all, including the preacher. But the preacher must first be convinced that divine grace applies to his or her own life in order to present it as efficacious to the individual life of each congregant, to the communal life of the congregation, and to the world. This is the unfailing and eternal good news that is the crux of the sermon.

In order to end with good news, the preacher begins with this focus. Starting with the text, the preacher identifies the action of God that is not only historical witness but that speaks of present action and expectant hope. A later chapter looks at methods for identifying good news in the biblical text, whether it is clearly visible in the text or not. Good news represents specific, recognizable, and transformative action that can be attributed to God's relationship with human beings. In order to meet the requirement of offering good news to the hearers, many students include statements in their sermon manuscripts that begin, "The good news of this sermon is. . . ." While identifying the good news of the sermon is a useful exercise for the preacher to test the contents of that sermon, there is no need to make this statement a part of the actual sermon. However, to facilitate the work of ensuring that the sermon contains good news, Allen suggests a simple formulaic exercise for preachers "to help them be sure that they are communicating good news from God in the congregation: summarize the main drift of the sermon in a single indicative sentence."[4]

In the process of developing the good news sermon, using a variation of Allen's model but starting with the biblical text, the preacher begins by formulating the good news of the text, also in a sentence in which the:

- subject is God (Christ/Holy Spirit)
- verb is the transformative action of God in human life
- predicate is the human result of divine/human interaction

The sentence thus formulated serves as the directive for creating the sermon and is used later to test that the sermon has fulfilled its purpose by meeting the stated directive. Once the good news statement has been created, the process of creating a good news sermon continues by connecting the good news of the text with the situation of the preaching context. Hearers will recognize it if the preacher has made the sermon's good news relevant to their situation. Although a definitive statement by the preacher may help to make it visible, if it does not emanate from scripture, if its content lacks substance, or if in the construction of the sermon the preacher has not made clear how it can transform and empower the hearers in their Christian living, no amount of emphasis will make it ring true. To facilitate the work of identifying and shaping good news for the sermon, I offer a simple three-step exercise. For ease of reference, I call it the *what, so what,* and *so that* of the good news.

EXERCISE 1: *WHAT* IS THE GOOD NEWS OF THE TEXT?

The good news of the sermon is a definitive word of divine grace that is retrieved from the text being preached and reframed to fit the context in which it is proclaimed. The preacher searches the substance of the text in order to unearth the specific offering of good news for the context of preaching. The good news statement is thus representative of the biblical text. Following are two examples of good news statements that are taken from the scripture passages noted, and that offer a substantive representation of divine grace in action.

Matthew 9:35–38
[35] Then Jesus went about all the cities and villages, teaching in their synagogues, and proclaiming the good news of the king-

dom, and curing every disease and every sickness. [36] When he saw the crowds, he had compassion for them, because they were harassed and helpless, like sheep without a shepherd. [37] Then he said to his disciples, "The harvest is plentiful, but the laborers are few; [38] therefore ask the Lord of the harvest to send out laborers into his harvest."

- Good news statement: Christ restores us to wholeness of life.
- Scriptural source: Matthew 9:35–36—Jesus went about all the cities and villages . . . curing every disease and every sickness.

The good news comes from Jesus' compassionate response to the needs of the people, healing them in body, mind, and spirit and so offering them wholeness of heart and life. Through Jesus' response to the needs of the people their situations are transformed and they are empowered to live in new ways. The good news selected from this text is readily apparent since the idea of God's compassion is readily recognizable as good news. However in many instances there are multiple representations of good news contained in a single text—for example the request for additional laborers may be presented as good news—and the preacher's choice of one will depend on the context in which the sermon is to be preached.

In some cases, as shown in the following example, the good news is not as overt, but still discernible in the text.

Jeremiah 29:1, 4–7
[1] These are the words of the letter that the prophet Jeremiah sent from Jerusalem to the remaining elders among the exiles, and to the priests, the prophets, and all the people, whom Nebuchadnezzar had taken into exile from Jerusalem to Babylon. . . . [4] Thus says the LORD of hosts, the God of Israel, to all the exiles whom I have sent into exile from Jerusalem to Babylon: [5] Build houses and live in them; plant gardens and eat what they produce. [6] Take wives and have sons and daughters; take wives for your sons, and give your daughters in marriage,

that they may bear sons and daughters; multiply there, and do not decrease. [7] But seek the welfare of the city where I have sent you into exile, and pray to the LORD on its behalf, for in its welfare you will find your welfare.

- Good news statement: God guides us even in our times of exile.

- Scriptural source: Jeremiah 29:4—Thus says the LORD of hosts, the God of Israel, to all the exiles whom I have sent into exile from Jerusalem to Babylon.

The message from God in the mouth of the prophet Jeremiah speaks of God's continued active concern for and involvement in the lives of the people, who are living in a state of exile. Through the prophet God directs the exiled people in the way that they should continue to live as people of the covenant. Through the good news of the covenantal love of God in action, the sermon offers the listening congregation a word of hope in the midst of their real life situations that make them exiles from their previous and expected lives.

In both cases, the scripture as good news offers God's grace in action; the good news may be used to bridge the historical realities of the cultures of the text and those of the present. Once it is identified, asking "so what?" of the good news allows the preacher to make it relevant to the context of the hearers of the sermon.

EXERCISE 2: ASK THE "SO WHAT?" QUESTION OF THE GOOD NEWS STATEMENT

Scripture provides evidence of God's redeeming love in history. Likewise the church maintains records of God's presence and power in the lives of individual Christians and the redeemed community over time. Yet these historical records are not the substance of the good news of the sermon. In a later chapter we will discuss the importance of contextualization for developing and preaching effective sermons; for now, it is enough to say that the good news one delivers needs to be directly related to the needs of the hearers. Asking a "so what?" question of the good news extracted from the text is one way of determining the appropriateness of the good news.

Why is this so? Because it helps to identify connections between the good news of the text and its impact on developing the hearers as Christian disciples. The good news statement is directed to the hearers and speaks of God's action in enabling them to live as Christians. The "so what?" question as the second step speaks to the specific needs of the particular hearers, the application of God's grace to those needs, and the hoped-for response of the hearers to the message of the sermon. The answer to the "so what?" question provides direction for the message or mission of the sermon. It directs the creation of a message statement that connects the good news of the sermon with the life of the hearers. Applying the "so what?" test to the good news statements developed in the first exercise may yield the following results:

- Scripture text: Matthew 9:35–38
- Good news statement: Christ restores us to wholeness of life
- Response to the "so what?" question: So that we can live full and abundant lives through Jesus Christ

The reason that the congregation needs to receive the good news of the restorative grace of God in Jesus Christ is that human sin has caused brokenness in human life and has fractured the divine/human relationship. In the text, this brokenness or sin is believed to be the direct cause of sickness and disease that Jesus has been healing. For the present congregation, Jesus Christ, God's gift of grace to all humanity, offers restoration to a full relationship with God and with all life. Even though there may not be the same belief in the connection between one's sin and physical sickness or disease, such restoration enables abundant living.

- Scripture text: Jeremiah 29:1, 4–7
- Good news statement: God guides us even in our times of exile
- Response to the "so what?" question: So that we can at all times look to God's guidance for our lives

Given the state of the world and of society in general, it is a safe assumption that there may be those present who feel exiled for what they consider normal behavior and who need someone to offer guidance for their life. The good news of God's guidance for the exiled Israelites may offer them a ray of hope and thus be good news for dealing with their situation of exile. As the congregation receives good news of divine presence in the situation of the text, they can also receive reassurance for their times of exile and alienation whether present or future. In addition, most, if not all, people experience moments when the issues of life cause them to feel adrift and the message that God's guiding presence is available in all times of crisis is good news.

The "so what?" question is intrinsic to the process of preaching and helps to interrogate the purpose and content of each sermon. Unless the sermon answers this question specifically, it will not connect directly with the congregation. Hearers of the sermon want to apply its message of good news to their individual lives. Answering the "so what?" question enables the preacher to ensure that it is appropriate to both text and context, and specifying the action to be taken in response to the good news allows the hearers to live into the transformative action of God's grace that the sermon presents.

The third and final step of this exercise is to develop a message statement. This statement names the action that the good news directs or supports in the hearers. It frames the purpose of the good news as a call to action, as an imperative statement that offers a directive for Christian living. It identifies the mission or purpose of the sermon and guides the hearers in applying the good news of the text, and ultimately of the sermon, through practical implementation in their lives.

EXERCISE 3: CREATE A MESSAGE STATEMENT *SO THAT* THE GOOD NEWS CAN LEAD TO DISCIPLESHIP.

The message statement is important in developing a good news sermon because it moves the good news forward into the life of the hearers by providing a call to action that affects or influences the hearers' lives as disciples of Jesus Christ. Good news preaching not only offers transformative good news to hearers, but also calls, invites, instructs, directs, or even urges hearers to move forward in living as disciples of Jesus Christ through the application of the good news in their lives. Creating a message statement early in the process of developing the sermon offers a goal toward which the preacher moves in the construction of the sermon. The message statement calls forth specific activity on the part of the hearers that is supported or even directed by the good news garnered from the text. It is purposeful and missional, and it gives evidence of the enabling grace of God in the divine/human relationship.

There is no specific formula for creating a message statement but, unlike the good news statement, the subject, whether named or implied, is human beings, and the verb is an imperative that invites action on the part of the hearers of the good news. In developing the message statement, students often connect the good news statement with the conjunctive phrase "so that" in order to arrive at a message statement that offers the hearers a direct explanation of the hoped-for action in their lives. This is a helpful response in determining the purpose of the sermon but it is more accurately the "so what?" response to the good news. The preacher must move beyond the "so what?" in order to name the hoped-for action by the hearers that is contained in the discipleship message. Following are suggested message statements created from the good news statements and the responses to the "so what?" question in the two previous exercises:

- Scripture text: Matthew 9:35–38
- Good news statement: Christ restores us to wholeness of life
- Response to the "so what?" question: So that we can live full and abundant lives through Jesus Christ.
- Message statement: Experience wholeness through Christ's presence in your life; go out and live abundantly

The purpose of the sermon: To provide the assurance that just as Christ responded with compassion to the needs of the biblical crowds, Christ will do the same for today's hearers as they confront the ills of life. This encourages the hearers' faith that they will experience wholeness of heart and life through Jesus Christ, which will in turn allow them to live an abundant life. The preacher makes clear in the sermon how one accepts and lives in the presence of Christ, the Christian meaning of wholeness of heart and life, and also what abundant living means for Christians.

- Scripture text: Jeremiah 29:1, 4–7
- Good news statement: God guides us even in our times of exile
- Response to the "so what?" question: So that we can at all times look to God's guidance for our lives
- Message statement: Be alert to God's leading and trust God to direct you in every situation

Purpose of the sermon: To connect with the feelings of exile that hearers are suffering and instill hope and courage in the congregation so that even when they feel lost and alone (as though exiled) they will trust that God continues to provide direction for their lives whatever the circumstances. It also is meant to provide assurance for others who, though they may not be experiencing such feelings at present, should they confront them in the future, can trust in God's guiding presence.

The exercise of naming *what* good news from the text will direct the sermon, determining its applicability to the context by means of the *"so what?"* question, and naming a specific charge *so that* the hearers will live into the sermonic good news, while essential to good news preaching, is not an exact science. It is simply an exercise that helps to ensure that the sermon is intentional in offering good news. Once the sermon is written, the preacher is encouraged to test its contents against this material and modify or change completely whatever is necessary to ensure that the sermon offers appropriate good news and a message that connects with the life of the hearers.

THE SOURCE OF THE GOOD NEWS

The source of the good news is always God. The good news derives not just from a single passage in the Bible but from the entire message of scripture and from the deepest theological beliefs of the church concerning God, Jesus Christ, and the Holy Spirit. Evidence of the grace of God is present in the words of scripture, and the preacher retrieves it and in some cases must struggle to decipher it in the midst of language that is often perverted and strange. But it is not the text itself, no matter how inspiring, that contains the good news. It is God working through the text to untangle the good news from the often convoluted streams of text and historical contexts; God working through the preacher to disengage beliefs and biases and to destroy filters that misappropriate or misinterpret the words of scripture; and God working through the people in the present and active contexts of their individual and corporate lives to bring to their attention the revelation and assurance of divine grace. It is God speaking that brings to life the Word of God that challenges, moves, or impels the hearers to connect with the good news in transforming ways. God in scripture and in life as lived in the present still speaks, and God is the source of the message of good news that must be delivered to the people. God, the originator, determines the content of the message that the preacher delivers.

The challenge for preachers is to hear correctly the message of God for the people. The preacher stands in the midst of the people and must also stand sufficiently apart from them in order to hear the Word of God that arises from the text that is being preached and that at the same time connects with the context in which it will be preached. In this way past and present connect through a divine word that transcends time and space, and the preacher gives voice to it in a way that can engage minds and hearts to hear the Word of God in all its fullness. God's word moves through history and into the present and is contextualized in the sermon to address the gathered community. Just as it does not emanate simply from the text, neither does it emanate simply from the community. The good news message of the sermon is not simply what the community wants to hear, but what it needs to hear to be delivered from sin and grow in grace.

Since I am advocating the idea of good news as the beginning point in the development of the sermon, I recommend strongly that preachers start by listening intently for the good news that needs to be delivered to the congregation. And since God is the source of the message, it behooves the preacher to listen to what God is saying to both preacher and people. Such active listening to God is part of good sermon preparation and facilitates the creation of a sermon that offers a message that impacts and even transforms the hearers as Christian disciples. The good news statement thus names the transformative action of divine love, whereas the message statement names the hoped-for response of the hearers to the divine love in action.

There is a singular point to every sermon, in whatever shape it is constructed, and that is to offer God's word of divine grace. The manner in which this word is couched is based on the art of the preacher, and the preacher's presentation either offers encouragement or causes the hearer to turn away from the word of truth. How the preacher understands the congregation's needs directly affects how the preacher interprets the biblical text. When the two meld, the preacher's words come to life as the divine word. In this way the preacher is not impelled to seek outside voices for some "good news" and is not tempted or driven to assume the dual role of source and authority of good news to the detriment of the sermon.

Edmund A. Steimle, responding to Karl Barth's statement that "[p]reaching is the Word of God which he himself has spoken," asks, "How is a preacher to determine the difference between his words and the Word of God?"[5] To do so the preacher must be engaged in active, ongoing communication with God in order to become familiar with God's voice, and thus be able to differentiate between words and Word. Yet the preacher is not the only one with whom God is communicating. For the good news to fit the people to whom it is proclaimed, the preacher must also be in communication with the people so that the words of the sermon can offer them an appropriate message of God's grace.

Often preachers are moved, inspired, and sometimes even compelled to call the people of God to an accounting of their sinful state as the biblical prophets did in their time. However, as prophets and like the biblical prophets, preachers today must also speak a word of hope, and above all, of divine love. Unless the sermon contains this, it cannot rightly be called the Word of God. At the same time, it is insufficient and unworthy of their prophetic role for preachers to speak only of God's grace without calling the people to an understanding of the sin that is mitigated by that grace, and the need for repentance, which is the evidence of their understanding and acceptance of God's grace. In light of the reality of human sin, God's unfailing grace made evident in the sermon makes the sermon a fit offering for the hearers.

Steimle speaks directly to this point when he questions "whether there are many congregations left today who listen dutifully and reverently to their minister's sermon as the Word of God which he himself has spoken."[6] Indeed, how can they and why should they if that purported Word of God contains no recognizable good news? And yet if the sermon is explicit in proclaiming God and specifically the love of God active and working transformatively in the lives of individuals and corporately in the life of the gathered community for the sake of the world, then they will hear the good news that they need and should expect from a sermon.

CENTERING THE SERMON IN GOOD NEWS

Making a general statement about God, such as "God loves" or "God wishes," is insufficient for offering transformative good news. Yes, God does love and God does wish; but unless the divine/human interaction is specific, it is unlikely to impact hearers as they move forward in their lives as redeemed Christians. In the same way, creating a good news statement that simply defines a divine characteristic, such as "God is love," is just as unhelpful in providing transformative good news. The action verbs suggested for use in a good news statement must speak clearly not only of God's continual work in the redemption of humanity but also of the transformation or empowerment it provides to those who have made the commitment to live into their identity as the redeemed children of God. The good news of God's saving action becomes more than a source of encouragement to the hearers, more than an invitation to continue on the path of Christian perfection. It offers the hearers confirmation of the enabling force of God's active presence and grace that facilitate their continued life in Christ and their continuing transformation leading to Christian perfection.

In presenting "A Brief Theology of Preaching," David Buttrick notes that "in our preaching Christ continues to speak to the church and through the church to the world. . . . Preaching is the preaching of Jesus Christ because it opens to us salvific new life and discloses the reality of God-toward-us."[7] With respect to good news preaching, what the preacher discloses is the reality of God-with-us in active participation in human endeavor that enables humanity to be both participants and exponents of God's grace. The sermon as purveyor of the message cannot shirk its responsibility of presenting divine grace in recognizable form. The preacher must make evident the offer of new life in a way that entices the engagement of hearers.

Earlier, I named the issue of the preacher engaging in communication with God as important and even critical to the preacher's ability to hear the divine word. Likewise it is necessary that the preacher have a defined theology of preaching. The basis of all interpretation of the biblical text must be theological, for it is through the lens of a preacher's theology that he or she understands God. Only by wrestling with the issues of divine presence is there the possibility or the hope that the words of scripture can become the Word of God for the people of God. In order to engage the text in a way that reveals the grace of God toward humanity, the preacher must be in harmony with the message of God that emanates from the biblical text.

The listening ear hears and interprets as the mind conceives. If the preacher does not understand God as grace, then the sermon is in jeopardy of being only useful, pastoral advice that is sorely lacking the incarnational spark necessary to make of ordinary persons witnesses and messengers of Christ. The Spirit of God must breathe life into both the preacher and the words of the sermon in order for them to become saturated with and transformed by God's grace. In this way the good news that began as a simple statement takes shape as the nucleus of the message and permeates all aspects of the sermon—content, creation, and delivery. As Fred Craddock explains, "If preaching is in any way a continuation into the present of God's revelation, then what we are doing and how we are doing it should be harmonious with our understanding of the mode of revelation. . . . In other words, from the transaction we call revelation we understand and implement the transaction we call preaching."[8] Preaching good news is the preacher's participation in the ongoing drama of human life that is rich and free through living fully in the grace of God.

THE HOLY SPIRIT AS AGENT OF GOOD NEWS

Preaching is impossible without the presence of the Holy Spirit. The sermon cannot be effective unless it is truly the Word of God, and that is not possible without the presence of the Holy Spirit. Like the bones in Ezekiel's vision, even with flesh and sinews, the sermon has no power to move the hearers without the breath of God giving it life. An effective sermon is founded on scripture, well constructed, theologically appropriate, contextual to its time and place, and delivered with conviction. It is good news presented by the preacher and received by the hearers for the continued growth of the body of Christ. This is a daunting task and it cannot be accomplished unless the Holy Spirit imbues the words and the preacher. In his farewell speech, Jesus promised the disciples that he would send the Holy Spirit to provide everything they needed to continue the work he had started (John 17:7–8), and the biblical witness tells of the outpouring of the promised Spirit on the day of Pentecost (Acts 2:1–21). We learn from scripture also that the grace of Christ gives the gifts necessary for the ongoing life of the church. Paul assures the Ephesians (4:7–16) that Christ has given varied gifts for building up the church for its work of ministry, and to the Corinthians he names the Holy Spirit as the source of all gifts (1 Cor. 12:1–11). Since Jesus Christ named the Holy Spirit as the one who would give power to the disciples for their work, we too can name the Holy Spirit as the source of power necessary to proclaim the word of God.

Paul implies that preachers have a special call from God (Romans 10), and that preaching itself is a spiritual gift, given by God and empowered by the Holy Spirit. As Marjorie Suchocki puts it, "God's word comes to us as a whisper. . . . It is not loud, like a clanging cymbal, nor is it boisterous, calling attention to itself. . . . To the contrary, it is a quiet word, a suggestive word, an inviting word, not always easily noticed."[9] Thus the preacher, called and gifted for the task, must listen intently for God's whispered message of hope and grace for the community. An earlier statement that bears repeating is that the preacher must be in active communication with God in order to hear the whispered message that

God sends to the people via the preacher.[10] Not only must the preacher listen to the initiating whispers of God, he or she must maintain that communication with the divine throughout the entire process of sermon development and look to the Holy Spirit as guide for the appropriate way of delivering the sermon. The Holy Spirit facilitates the church's hearing of the good news that exists in all of scripture and makes of the preaching event a moment of worship and celebration for the people of God.

James Forbes believes that "the person who preaches the gospel makes a statement about the Holy Spirit just by entering the pulpit."[11] Like Forbes, I believe that through divine-human communication the Holy Spirit guides the preacher in the selection of the biblical text for preaching, whether or not the lectionary is followed. Such divine guidance takes into consideration the needs of both preacher and people and directs the preacher through all the steps of preparing for preaching. Long before thoughts become words or phrases or sounds, it is the Holy Spirit that prompts preachers in the direction that the sermon needs to follow. In order to facilitate the agency of the Holy Spirit, preachers must allow sufficient time for meditation on scripture, for prayer and personal devotion, and even for silent reflection and active listening for the divine voice. Active listening through spoken prayer and silent reflection helps preachers to recognize God's voice as they prepare to speak God's Word.

So how does one recognize the voice of God? How does one become attuned to the presence of the Holy Spirit in the development and preaching of the sermon? The preacher who has been in communication with God will understand the need to test the thoughts of the mind and the inclinations of the heart in the light of God's love for all people. In other words, if the preacher's message focuses exclusively on leveling accusations of sin without offering the mitigating grace of God, it is unlikely that the message originated from the Holy Spirit. The Holy Spirit as the power of God is the promised gift of Christ to comfort, support, and sustain the people of God. It is offered because of the need for God's grace, intrinsic to all human life, and the Holy Spirit speaks the divine word into the truth of human fallibility. Likewise, if the preacher seeks to bypass the reality of sin in a misguided effort to spare the people from facing their humanness, the news offered as good is worthless. The Holy Spirit speaks into and against the reality of sin and offers a redemptive word in all circumstances. The preacher who listens for this dual focus is assured in the hearing: it is the voice of God.

Forbes reminds us that the preacher must be anointed for the task of preaching. He cites the anointing of Jesus "as a model of spiritual formation,"[12] and notes the common though erroneous belief that anointing is a one-time event. The preacher needs the anointing of the Holy Spirit for every occasion of preaching and at every step in the process of developing and preaching the sermon. Jesus himself claimed the anointing of God for his own ministry (Luke 4:16–22) and the preacher needs the same in order to create and deliver each sermon. Thus anointed by the Holy Spirit, the preacher is empowered to be God's representative and can fulfill the role of messenger of God. This anointing is not the result of critical study of the biblical text, or of superior hermeneutical or theological knowledge. It is a gift of God. Preachers who open themselves to God experience this grace more readily. With Jesus as a model, the preacher's life is open and available to God to be used for the building up of the church. Just as Jesus' anointing was not for his own sake, so too the anointing of the preacher is not for personal gain or acclamation, but for the church.

As the agent of good news, the Holy Spirit is present with the gathered community—preacher and hearers—and the event of preaching in the midst of the community may be recognized as one aspect of the broader work of the Spirit to nurture, empower, and guide the church so that it may serve Christ in its service to the world. The people as hearers play as active a part in the preaching task as the preacher, given the conversations between God and the preacher, God and the people, and the preacher and the people. The relationship between God and the people is as informative for the preacher in determining the substance of the sermon as is the preacher's own conversation with God. Through the preacher's conversation with the people, the Holy Spirit speaks into being the message of good news that is appropriate to the needs of the people in that particular time and place.

THE SERMON AS GOOD NEWS IN THE CONTEXT OF WORSHIP

In the same way that the Holy Spirit calls and empowers the preacher for the task, so too the Holy Spirit gathers the people for worship, which includes the preaching and hearing of God's word. Worship is the people's response to God's self-revelation in the midst of the gathered community. To my mind, that includes preaching. As good news of God's grace, the sermon is evidence of God's self-revelation and therefore worthy of the celebrative response of the gathered community. Celebration of God's presence in all of life is intrinsic to the act of worship for which the people of God gather. The experience and rituals of worship enable the people of God to give voice in praise and acclamation to being recipients of God's grace, and the sermon is one representation of that voice.

Frank Thomas, following in the footsteps of his mentor Henry Mitchell, studied the role of celebration in African American preaching.[13] He looks back to "the early New Testament community (that) understood Jesus Christ himself to be the good news"[14] and therefore worthy of celebrating whenever the church gathered. In describing this celebrative motif of African American preaching, Thomas focuses on the good news of Jesus' salvific act as the source and reason for celebration in the sermon. However, his focus on the second Testament leaves one wondering whether good news is not also found in the first Testament.

The celebration of God's grace begins with creation and continues throughout biblical history. It is present in the law and the prophets in God's covenantal love for the Hebrew people, a constant amidst their human failures, such as constant wandering away from the worship of Yahweh and rejection of God's directives. God's presence, protection, and grace throughout scripture evoke a celebrative response from all who live within that legacy. That response is not contingent on a celebrative style of sermon, but the preacher who understands that sermons celebrate God's grace will make sure that celebration defines its message. People's celebration in response to the good news that they have received is an act of worship. It may be initiated or continued through the preached sermon, and the response of the hearers may be evidenced in changed lives that result in more faithful discipleship. Preaching is thus a celebrative act of God's people, which helps to shape and define the ongoing life of the gathered community.

Preaching is liturgical because preaching occurs only in the context of worship. Too often, regardless of the situation or context, the delivery of an unwanted message is referred to as preaching. And while it may be too late to reclaim this colloquial definition from the untutored minds within and outside of the church, the preacher has the opportunity to remind the church that it is the agent of proclamation of God's message of salvation. Proclaiming a message of good news in every sermon may begin to remove the stigma that seems to surround the activity of preaching because it means being faithful to the eternal grace of God revealed in all of scripture and calls Christians of every age and stage of life to a celebrative response of worship and praise.

By being intentional and explicit about proclaiming good news, the sermon offers its hearers a glimpse into the mind of God, which accepts each person and offers to each unending grace. The sermon is good news when it connects and reconnects the people of God with the assurance of God's presence as the fulfillment of the divine/human covenant and, above all, when it enables the people of God through worship to acknowledge and confess the presence of God in all the vagaries of their human lives. The preacher delves into the words of scripture to unearth the word of life to share with the people in a particular time and place. The sermon *is* good news when God's presence with preacher and people is not only instructive but empowering.

two

◼

Laying the Biblical Foundations
for the Good News

i t was the first evening of the basic preaching class and, in the process of reviewing the syllabus, I repeated a statement that was printed as one of the goals of the class: that by the completion of the term, students should understand the Bible as foundational to preaching. A challenge came from a student who had seemed to become more and more troubled as I explained the contents of the syllabus. This student considered my statement problematic and stated that he could produce a good sermon based on the writer Thoreau. I disagreed. Having listened to too many sermons that were short on scripture or lacking it entirely, I know that there are those who hold the same belief as that student expressed that we may construct a sermon based on something other than scripture.

That I consider scripture foundational for preaching does not dismiss or diminish the place of other materials in the sermon. Indeed, the inclusion of nonbiblical material can add greater depth and clarity to our understanding of the biblical word. However, since we believe that scripture is the Word of God, and that the preacher is charged to offer the Word of God to the people, then it stands to reason that the sermon should begin with what has already been accepted as the inspired Word of God. And although scholars have long debated the inerrancy of the biblical texts, this does not diminish the divine inspiration that brought the Bible into being and that is necessary to create the sermon.

The preacher engages scripture to discern its relevance as the Word of God for particular people in a particular time and place. Having faithfully delved into the text and unearthed its meaning for preaching, the preacher becomes the vessel by which the gospel is proclaimed, and the words of the sermon become the medium through which the Word of God is delivered to the people. Homileticians and preachers in general have accepted that only through divine mystery can the words spoken by the preacher become the Word of God, and only as the Word of God can the words of the sermon be effective in transforming the minds and hearts of the hearers. As Eugene Lowry puts it, "preaching the sermon is a *task*; proclaiming the Word is the hoped-for *goal*."[1] The ability of that task to reach its goal, however, is partly dependent on the preacher's ability to search deeply into the words of scripture and impart its truth to the gathered congregation. Biblical interpretation lays a foundation on which to support the accuracy or appropriateness of the good news of the sermon. Analyzing how the good news might speak into the situation of those to whom it is being delivered is equally necessary.

This chapter looks at how we approach the scripture text to identify the good news and interpret it for our context. In order to appropriate the good news of the text for the context of preaching, both text and context require interpretation or exegesis. In the exegetical process, I give as much attention to unearthing good news from scripture for the preaching context as I do to interpreting the context in which the scripture will be preached. In this way, the interpretive work of exegesis connects the content of the scripture text or texts with the people of God in the present. Also as part of this interpretive process, I determine the style or structure of the sermon. The choice of sermon style includes an analysis of the context in which the sermon will be preached. This is critical when one is a guest preacher, but it is also important for the pastor/preacher who is addressing a familiar congregation. The host congregation might ask a guest preacher to address a particular theme in light of a special event in the church. That may be done through the lens of a particular scripture passage or by applying the theme more widely using several texts. On the other hand, the pastor/preacher may follow the lectionary readings for weekly sermons but must still choose the text most suited to the congregation's need of the moment. Whatever the reason for the preacher's selection of sermon type and scripture text or texts, ensuring that the sermon offers good news that emanates from scripture and that is applicable to the hearers necessitates interpretation of both text and context.

SERMON TYPES—EXPOSITORY OR TOPICAL

In concert with the interpretive work of text and context, the preacher decides on the type of sermon type for the occasion—expository or topical. An expository sermon breaks open a text, allowing the interpretation of the text to be applied to the context and showing its relevance for that congregation. A topical sermon brings light to a particular topic or theme (such as God's faithfulness) and reveals its applicability to the moment of preaching.

In expository preaching, the purpose of the sermon is to help the congregation interpret its situation through the lens of a biblical passage. The development of the sermon centers in the exegesis, theological analysis, and hermeneutical appropriation of the biblical material. John McClure emphasizes the centrality and the authority of scripture for the expository sermon. "First, preachers strive to understand the biblical text on its own terms as much as possible apart from their own personal or doctrinal agendas. . . . [S]econd, [they strive for] clarity in communication."[2] Yet the focus on scripture cannot distract the preacher from ensuring that its intrinsic good news comes alive or showing its relevance to the present.

In topical preaching, the preacher helps the congregation interpret a topic from the perspective of the gospel. Topical sermons typically address a Christian doctrine or practice, a personal or social situation. The topical sermon has a biblical foundation, but it does not center on the exposition of a biblical text in the same way as the expository sermon. Instead, it is the people's needs that direct the preacher's attention to the topic and then engages it theologically and biblically. Because it connects directly with congregational needs many preachers use topical preaching for special occasions in the life of the congregation. Although the initial focus is different from the expository sermon, topical sermons also require a foundation of a biblical text, but Ronald Allen offers this cautionary word against bringing together unrelated texts under the banner of a particular topic, warning that "in all cases the integrity of the Bible is to be honored."[3]

The biblical record of God's covenantal relationship and God's direct and indirect action in the lives of human beings offers a window through which people can see and understand God's unwavering presence and grace in human life. But while the Bible speaks clearly of God's presence, its truths are often hidden in the cobwebs of history and language and interpretation, so the preacher's task is to decipher its context and meaning. Even today, the Bible brings a relevant word and is a continuing source of revelation of God's everlasting presence in the world. The preacher's decision on sermon type depends on the preaching context and the people's needs. For example, the preacher may give a series of expository sermons to develop biblical knowledge in a congregation that resists the discipline of Bible study. Likewise a series of topical sermons may serve to address the overall subject of discipleship, mission, or some other Christian doctrine or practice. Once the preacher has decided, he or she selects the supporting text or texts and begins the task of interpretation. A preacher begins the exegetical process for both the expository and the topical sermon by identifying the good news and the context in which the sermon will be preached and heard. In other words, how the preacher interprets the biblical text depends on the human context of the preaching moment.

EXEGESIS: AN INTERPRETIVE PROCESS

Biblical exegesis is about offering a critical explanation or interpretation of a biblical text. It requires that the reader delve deeply into the scripture passage to unearth its meaning. In one of his early texts, Ronald Allen describes biblical exegesis as "concerned with recovering the historical background of the text."[4] In a later text he expands his definition of the term to be "the disciplined process of locating the possible meanings of a text in its historical, literary, and theological contexts."[5] In both cases, his definition refers to the process of peeling back the layers of history surrounding the location within which the text has been anchored in order to offer it in the present as the biblical word. Biblical exegesis thus offers a snapshot of biblical history.

What did the text mean in its original context? What situation caused the text to be written? What is the situation of which the text speaks? What is the text's literary form and how does that influence our reading and understanding of the text? A preacher asks these and many other questions as part of the historical analysis. The historical picture is revelatory—with respect to the good news of divine grace and to the way in which the people represented in the text understood the nature of God and their place in the divine plan. Such exegetical work also identifies the first hearers of the text and the place and function of the text in their lives. More important for good news preaching, biblical exegesis works to uncover the layers of history between which lie the essence of the divine/human encounter and its silent witness to God's eternal grace.

The answers to the historical questions may challenge the preacher at many levels and may lure the preacher to bypass the historical reality of the text in favor of a more palatable interpretation. However, beyond its historicity, the literary form of the text may suggest or determine how it is preached. Its literary construction, key words, and historical exigencies may have significant influence on sermonic form and content. In addition, a preacher's inability to research or review the text in its original language may obscure meaning that does not translate clearly in modern-day English. Yet somehow the past must meet the present; the preacher must be able to unpack the text and offer its good news for each occasion of preaching.

When the intent of preaching is to offer transformative good news to the hearers, we broaden the exegetical process to include not only interpreting the text or topic but also the context of preaching to determine the nature of good news that will be appropriate and applicable to the hearers. In the same way we investigate each text to bring to light its full meaning, so too we investigate the congregation to unearth the historical and present situations that will affect the people's ability to hear and take to heart the good news. The context of preaching requires specific interpretive attention because it is the connection between text and context that gives substance to the offering of divine grace in the sermon.

On occasion, the preacher may engage a topic for preaching during the investigation of a particular biblical text, such as the issue of faith in the process of healing, as seen in one of Jesus' healing miracles recorded in the gospels. In such a case the selection of the text precedes the choice of preaching topically as the style of the sermon and the exegesis of the text ensures that the emergent topic is actually contained in or relevant to the text. On the other hand, many topical sermons are focused on a particular Christian doctrine or practice; however, the foundation of ecclesial doctrines is theological, and in most cases it is also biblical, therefore the preacher uses one or more texts in the process of interpreting the topic. When the preacher begins with the topic he or she determines the good news that is relevant for the hearers based on both theological investigation and the context of the hearers. Only when this topical analysis is done should the preacher select scriptures that engage the topic and become the basis of the good news preached.

HOMILETICAL EXEGESIS

In teaching exegesis for preaching, I use the term homiletical exegesis as a way of including both exegesis of the biblical text or the topic and the context in which the sermon will be preached. Homiletical exegesis follows a methodology similar to biblical interpretation, and indeed borrows from it. However, it begins with an awareness of the present situation of the congregation that not only sheds light on the applicability of the biblical or topical interpretation, but also gives insight as to the good news that needs to be shared with the hearers.

Homiletical exegesis for good news preaching includes historical, literary, and theological methodologies of biblical interpretation, and combines biblical interpretation and contextual analysis in order to give the preacher an authentic platform from which to launch the sermonic message of good news to the people of God. It assumes that the preacher accepts scripture as the true record of God's presence in human endeavors and has a sound theology that acknowledges the covenantal grace of God as an affirming, enlivening love that is available to all people.

Prerequisite to the basic preaching class at my seminary are introductory courses in both Testaments, where students are taught appropriate methods of biblical interpretation. In addition students are encouraged to take at least one theology course that serves to anchor their understanding of God as they encounter various aspects of the divine nature in scripture. Also, because homiletical exegesis is a combination of biblical exegesis and contextual analysis, a basic pastoral care course may be beneficial for understanding the context of the congregation. However, it is the preacher's commitment to offering good news that facilitates the creation of a sermon that encourages Christian discipleship, or that calls nonbelievers to become disciples of Jesus Christ. That is prerequisite to the overall exegetical process.

In order to accomplish genuine good news preaching through the exposition of a chosen text or topic, the preacher begins at the place of anticipation, where the hope of promise is met with the reality of fulfillment. That means that the process of homiletical exegesis does not begin with the interrogation of the text to identify its good news, but with the anticipation or expectation that there is good news in the text or topic for preaching. I typically approach homiletical exegesis for good news sermons by addressing three sets of questions directed at:

1. Identification of good news—recognizable or hidden in the text or the topic

2. Interpretation of the biblical text or the topic—the historical, literary, and other critical elements that facilitate recognition of good news in the text or topic

3. Analysis of the congregation—the situation of preaching and the specific shape or content of the good news it requires

Systematic biblical and contextual interpretation enables the preacher to appropriately apply the substance of the text in its contextual framework, and therefore it is important to develop a discipline of exegetical work for every sermon. When the preacher neglects the interpretive work, the sermon is often rudderless and drifts away from the scripture passage it is meant to expound. On the other hand, when the preacher takes study exegesis and turns it into sermon exegesis, the sermon becomes a paper or report; it ceases to be a sermon that either offers good news or presents the Word of God. Homiletical exegesis allows scripture to speak and offer good news appropriate to the context of the sermon, whether expository or topical. The step-by-step process for homiletical exegesis for good news sermons provided in appendix A may be used as a handout for students and as a working document by preachers.

IDENTIFICATION OF GOOD NEWS

The process of naming the good news is similar for both expository and topical sermons: unearthing or revealing the evidence of divine grace that speaks to the situation of the hearers. Although the word "gospel"—translated as "good news"—is associated generally with Jesus Christ as fulfillment of the messianic promise, the preacher should resist the temptation to read Jesus into the Old Testament, especially because the word gospel in its generic meaning as good news can be applied legitimately to the whole Bible. In a recent class several students assured me that in their denominations it would be anathema not to end every sermon by naming Jesus Christ, whether or not their preaching text had come from the New Testament. This challenged me to find a way to move First Testament sermons into the Second Testament in a way that maintained the integrity of the interpretative process.

While the great good news is our redemption through Jesus Christ, there is always available good news that is representative of the enabling grace of God in the lives of the people of God. Likewise, the grace of God is not a concept that came into being with the apostolic church, but was present and operating from the beginning of human history. Thus exegeting each biblical text for good news means beginning with the theological understanding that the nature of God is above all one of grace. In a similar way, regardless of one's theological stance or the particular divine attribute that one affirms, the basic foundation of theology is the goodness of God. In any context or theological position, this is good news and is the foundation on which all authentic Christian doctrines and practices stand. Therefore it is the beginning point in identifying the good news in the topic. Similarly the action of applying the good news to Christian life is the same for both expository and topical sermons. These steps may help to identify and apply the good news in both types of sermons:

1. Addressing the Text or Topic
   - Approach the text or topic with prayerful expectation of finding good news.
   - Allow the Holy Spirit free rein in revealing the divine presence.

2. Finding the Theological Meaning
   - What does the text or topic say about God and the divine/human relationship?
   - Connect the revelation of the divine biblically and/or theologically with the congregational situation.
   - Identify the divine action that speaks of human transformation.

3. Naming the Good News
   - Using the biblical text or theological representation of the topic, develop a good news statement using the following format (detailed in chapter 1):
     - subject is God (Christ/Holy Spirit)
     - verb is the transformative action of God in human life
     - predicate is the human result of divine/human interaction
   - Test the good news statement with the contents or background of the scripture passage or the theological representation to verify that it represents human transformation or empowerment for discipleship.

4. Develop a Message Statement
   - Ask the "so-what?" question of the good news to determine the applicability of the good news of the text to the context of the hearers.

- Create a message statement that names the action of Christian discipleship that the good news empowers or facilitates.

An explanation of this process and its three-step exercise are included in chapter 1 in the section entitled "The Importance of Naming Good News in the Sermon."

INTERPRETATION OF THE BIBLICAL TEXT OR THE TOPIC

The interpretive process of homiletical exegesis seeks to unearth the elements of text or topic that are critical to developing and offering good news in the sermon. For the expository sermon, the activity of interpretation is located in a single text from which the preacher has identified and extracted good news that speaks to the present context. The topical sermon necessitates interpreting the topic to determine its applicability for the moment of preaching first, then interpreting the biblical text or texts to ensure their appropriateness to the topic and to each other. To avoid inappropriate proof-texting, critically interpreting the biblical texts used in preaching the topic is particularly important.

Biblical interpretation allows the text to be heard in its own language and its own images to be seen. Such exegesis brings to light important nuances in the text, and through it the preacher delves as deeply as possible into the biblical record to determine its meaning and focus historically in as many time periods as is relevant for applying it to the present. Some of the most common methods of biblical interpretation are:[6]

- *Historical critical method* uses textual criteria, engaging the text in its original language, and looks at the historical background, the literary context, and the form and function of the text in the ideology of the ancient world. This method is descriptive, not theological.

- *Literary criticism* looks at the way in which the form and construction of the text shapes its meaning. Whether the form is identifiable as narrative, saga, myth, legend, historical narrative, dialogue, parable, or some other form, literary criticism addresses the question of its interpretation for theological understanding.

- *Form criticism* considers the intrinsic shape or form of the text. It is approached by identifying the genre of literature in order to determine the original purpose of the text and its underlying or layers of theological meaning.

- *Redaction criticism* looks at the way in which the redactor as editor used the text to express theological beliefs. This method is historical and is focused on determining the author's purpose in writing the text in order to unearth its meaning and purpose in scripture.

The preacher may use any of these methodologies in the interpretive process. The preacher concentrates on learning about the text in its biblical context, but is charged to include in the sermon only those elements of the text that bear directly on the contemporary concern that the sermon addresses. Following is an example of interpretive material applicable to the texts of Matthew 9:35–38 and Jeremiah 29:1, 4–7, based on the good news and message statements developed in chapter 1:[7]

Matthew 9:35–38

[35] Then Jesus went about all the cities and villages, teaching in their synagogues, and proclaiming the good news of the kingdom, and curing every disease and every sickness. [36] When he saw the crowds, he had compassion for them, because they were harassed and helpless, like sheep without a shepherd. [37] Then he said to his disciples, "The harvest is plentiful, but the laborers are few; [38] therefore ask the Lord of the harvest to send out laborers into his harvest."

- Good news statement: Christ restores us to wholeness of life.

- Message statement: Experience wholeness through Christ's presence in your life; go out and live abundantly.

- Homiletical exegesis (summarized): Verse 35 is a summary statement that marks a transition in Jesus' ministry between the healing miracles recorded in the previous chapter and the charge to the disciples. This one verse summarizes the work that Jesus has been about as he accomplishes those tasks for which he says he came as Luke (4:16–20) describes it. Matthew's language is specific to belief in Jesus as the Messiah, the true shepherd of the people. His gospel is believed to have been written to instruct the church community in their own faith. His church had carried out an unsuccessful mission to the Jews and he no longer saw these uncommitted persons as potential disciples but rather as harassed and helpless, being misled by synagogue leaders. He understood that the present and future of the church was dependent on non-Jews—Gentiles—and needing leadership in the church community to spread the message of Christ. The text is a narrative composed by its author and based on material adapted from the Gospel of Mark. The story is designed for reading to the whole church community and reminds them of Jesus' compassion—not condemnation—for Israel. The text is appropriate to the church today in the context of society's ills, declining congregations, and masses of unchurched persons (sheep without a shepherd) needing the compassionate touch of Christ.

Jeremiah 29:1, 4–7

¹ These are the words of the letter that the prophet Jeremiah sent from Jerusalem to the remaining elders among the exiles, and to the priests, the prophets, and all the people, whom Nebuchadnezzar had taken into exile from Jerusalem to Babylon. ⁴ Thus says the LORD of hosts, the God of Israel, to all the exiles whom I have sent into exile from Jerusalem to Babylon: ⁵ Build houses and live in them; plant gardens and eat what they produce. ⁶ Take wives and have sons and daughters; take wives for your sons, and give your daughters in marriage, that they may bear sons and daughters; multiply there, and do not decrease. ⁷ But seek the welfare of the city where I have sent you into exile, and pray to the LORD on its behalf, for in its welfare you will find your welfare.

- Good news statement: God guides us even in our times of exile.

- Message statement: Be alert to God's leading and trust God to direct you in every situation.

- Homiletical exegesis (summarized): This is part of a prophetic oracle presented as a letter from Jeremiah to the exiles that have been deported to Babylon. This portion of the letter has a distinct message. It reminds the exiles that God is the one responsible for sending them into exile and advises the exiles to accept their fate and make the best of their situation. The situation is punishment from God, but their redemption lies in their ability not only to come to terms with their situation, but also to do good in the place of their captivity. It rests on the assurance of God's presence with them even in their captivity and invites them to be part of the blessing of God in a foreign land. The prophetic voice with which Jeremiah speaks to the exiles brings a message that is difficult to hear given the nationalistic nature of the people. It calls the people back to their covenantal relationship with Yahweh (pray) even in the midst of the devastation of their lives caused by their exile from Jerusalem. Instead of prayers of deliverance from Babylon, they are instructed (by God) to intercede on behalf of their captor (Babylon), which speaks of God's presence and direction even in the times when it seems that God is far away. Although theirs is physical exile, it was caused by their spiritual disobedience (self-exile from the covenant). The text offers to present-day people the reminder and assurance that whether self-imposed or suffered because of issues beyond their control, God is present with the people of God in their times of spiritual and physical suffering (exile). Further, regardless of the circumstances, God offers a word to guide our lives when we feel exiled from God and from all that is familiar in our lives.

The selection of interpretive material for use in the sermon is based directly on the focus of the good news. The choice of material to be included in the sermon hinges on both the good news and the message of the sermon. It is not intended to show the entire history or meaning of the selected text, the section of scripture from which it is taken, or the biblical book of which it is a part. The preacher's focus is determined by the intersection of text and context with respect to its contents as good news and a message of Christian discipleship.

If the sermon is topical, the preacher interprets the topic to determine whether it fits the context of the life of the church theologically, doctrinally, or liturgically. The preacher may begin by addressing one of the doctrines of the church or a particular aspect of an established Christian practice. What is important is that the topic must be specific enough to connect directly with the hearers as individuals. For example, the church may be involved in a stewardship campaign and the pastor may choose to preach on the topic of Christian service as a way of encouraging the members to recognize their gifts and the purpose of their gifts in the life and work of the church. For good news preaching the preacher begins by addressing two questions of each topic:

- What is the good news of the topic?
- Does the good news of the topic offer an appropriate message to the situation of the hearers?

For example, on the topic of Christian service, the preacher may focus on the Holy Spirit as the source of the gifts that enable one's service, thereby helping hearers to understand that their gifts are not of their own creation and that they are given by God for a specific purpose, namely, for the building up of the church.

Unlike biblical interpretation, there are no specific methodologies for this work, but applying a theological framework of questions allows the preacher to determine the credibility of the topic. The following questions (applied to the topic of Christian service) facilitate this theological investigation:

1. Is the topic theologically sound?

- Most preachers identify with a particular theological position and are likely to choose a topic that fits that position.
- In preparing to address the topic the preacher is helped by investigating other theological positions that may bring light to appropriate treatment of the topic. (Christ calls his disciples to be of service in the kingdom of God.)

2. Is the topic representative of Christian tradition, doctrine, or practice?

- Generally topical sermons address some aspect of Christianity, such as tradition, doctrine, or practice. Unfortunately this does not guarantee that the topic is representative of an acceptable belief or form of Christian discipleship.
- The history and use of the topic across Christendom help to determine its usefulness in guiding the congregation in their discipleship. (There is a recognized tradition of missional service in the Christian church in the name of Christ.)

3. Is the topic appropriate to biblical history and tradition?

- Since scripture is foundational to all sermons, it is important that biblical reference be readily available for inclusion in the sermon.
- There may be several and differing positions on the topic in the Bible.
- Applying the particular aspect of the topic for preaching will help to guide the selection of biblical references. (There are several examples of persons dedicated to Christian service recorded in the New Testament, especially in Acts of the Apostles, for example, Dorcas [Acts 9:36–42] and Lydia [Acts 16:13–15].)

4. Is the topic doctrinally appropriate?

- Even when a congregation names itself nondenominational, it is directed by commonly held Christian doctrines and mores.
- The traditions common to Christianity provide a measure for determining the appropriateness of the topic beyond specific

denominational or congregational beliefs or practices. (The content or measure of Christian service as developed in the sermon differs according to the particular context but has common understanding in Christian history and practice. This may include the work of preachers, teachers, evangelists, missionaries, or other ministries and workers in the church.)

5. ARE THERE PAST EXPERIENCES WITH THIS TOPIC THAT MAY IMPACT ITS HEARING?

- Pastoral wisdom guides the selection and approach to addressing the topic in the particular context.
- The experience of members is only one aspect of this investigation. Concern for the experience of the wider community, for society in general, and even across human history also helps determine how suitable the topic is for preaching. (The current understanding, history, and practice of service in the congregation will help direct the content of "Christian service" expounded in the sermon. The ministry areas of the church, both past and present, provide information and direction on the types of service applicable to the needs of the congregation that may be presented in the sermon.)

ANALYSIS OF THE CONGREGATION

By taking time to consider the congregation, the preacher is better able to frame the good news in such a way that people in the pews can connect with it. Taking time to address the specific needs of the people will yield its own rewards in the response of the people. The congregation expects and is entitled to receive the good news of the gospel. Be aware of the situations that exist within the life of the congregation, but avoid the temptation of speaking to those situations through the sermonic text. Maintain the focus of the message on the good news of the gospel and its essential role in the formation of Christian discipleship, and expect the congregation to respond in different and new ways to each message. For example, the sermon on Christian service will be more affirming and inspiring if the examples name actual ministries in the church.

The congregation's level of biblical literacy, their knowledge and understanding of scripture, and their theological stance have significant impact on the way that they will receive the good news and respond to the message of the sermon. How they understand God, the church, and their specific congregation are as important as the culture of their community, their social and political realities. The level of activity and participation in the life and witness of the church also affects their hearing of good news and directly correlates to their response as Christian disciples. Again using the example of the topical sermon on Christian service, if in addition to preaching about it, the pastor/preacher offers a study on the topic that showcases biblical examples of service to Christ and the church, this will help the congregation to receive the message more deeply and strengthen the invitation to give of their service to the church.

The situation of the preaching moment, whether the sermon is for a regular worship service or a special event in the life of the congregation, also has significance for preaching good news, and the expectations of the congregation vary depending on the type of worship service and its place in the liturgical life of the congregation. In addition, the relationship between the preacher and congregation, whether or not it is ongoing or one time, makes a difference in the reception of the sermonic message. At times a visiting preacher may be more successful in addressing a difficult matter or preaching a difficult message to the congregation than the assigned pastor. Congregational dynamics, which involve the issue of leadership—both laity and clergy—the application of denominational polity, the structure of committees and groups, and the relationship of age-level groups all play a part in shaping the context for preaching and enabling the hearers to receive and respond to the message of good news.

Whether the process of homiletical exegesis is undertaken for an expository or a topical sermon, the preacher benefits from following a systematic approach with specific guidelines and questions for interpreting the biblical text for preaching, and that includes the analysis of the preaching context.

A PROCESS FOR EXEGETING THE EXPOSITORY SERMON[8]

While I do not intend to offer an expansive presentation on either biblical interpretation or congregational analysis, I have found the following steps in this process to be an effective approach to homiletical exegesis; however, it assumes the preacher's familiarity with common methodologies of biblical interpretation. The process is facilitated by a list of questions, included in appendix B, that are directed to retrieving the necessary information. These suggestions help the preacher engage the process and are not rigid rules to be followed without question.

1. MEET THE TEXT

   - Approach the text with expectation. Be open and prepared to hear something new from the text.

   - Read the text with a listening attitude. Read the text aloud several times, each with a different emphasis if possible.

   - Engage as many senses as possible and give your emotions free rein. Listen for the good news that arises from the text. Listen for its message on discipleship. Listen for words that seem significant.

2. ESTABLISH THE BOUNDARIES OF THE TEXT IN ITS IMMEDIATE AND LARGER CONTEXTS IN THE BIBLE

   - Establish the boundaries of the text. Does the passage seem connected or disconnected from the surrounding text?

   - Determine the literary form and how it affects the meaning of the text. Identify and determine the significance of its authorship and placement in the greater corpus.

   - Establish the plain sense of the text, that is, what is the surface meaning of the text? What do the words themselves seem to say? Does everything in the text make sense? Look for changes in setting, characters, and theme.

   - How does the meaning of particular words or phrases help establish the meaning of the text? Note items from an introduction to the book that might be important for interpreting this passage.

- Check whether this is a layered passage, that is, is this a narrative, is this a single story, or are there multiple layers of story or plot written into or hidden in the text?

3. LOCATE THE TEXT HISTORICALLY

- Determine the historical setting of the text. Ask the introductory questions: Who was the author? Where was the text written? When was it written? For what purpose was it written?

- Identify the biblical history. How many biblical periods affect the meaning of this text? Parables, for example, are presented according to the context of the gospel writer but are referential to Jesus' time when the parable was told originally.

- Determine the author's intention in writing this passage to a particular audience. Is the author trying to confirm or challenge the views of the reader?

- Establish the dynamics that were important to the community to whom the text was written. What are the social, cultural, political, and religious realities that affected the way in which the text was written and presented to the original hearers?

4. EVALUATE THE LITERARY FORM

- Identify the form of the text and its influence on how the text is read. Does its form—as narrative/nonnarrative, saga, myth, legend, historical narrative, scholastic writing, dialogue, law, prophecy, parable, or other—hold intrinsic meanings for the interpretation of the text?

- What are the bridge words that move the message of the text along and how do they give particular meaning to the sequencing of the action contained in the text?

- Which words have history that bears further examination or requires additional research into their origins?

- Does the form of the text offer or dictate a particular model for the sermon?

5. Engage the Text for Preaching

- Consult a reliable commentary or other interpretive source. Use the commentary to expand or deepen your ideas rather than taking the ideas or suggestions as the framework for your sermon.

- Based on historical findings and an initial analysis, what are the issues that present themselves? What insights from commentaries complement and supplement your own?

- Synthesize and narrow your focus as you begin thinking about preaching on this passage. Allow the theological, existential, experiential issues you identified to focus your interpretation of the text.

- What imagery is used and what is its impact? Do the biblical images suggest appropriate imagery for the present? How are the characters portrayed and how do they interact?

6. Contextualize the Text for the Present

- Connect the text with the present. How do the social, cultural, political, and religious situations of the text compare to the present? How do they inform our understanding of the meaning and use of the text in preaching?

- Do characters and their portrayal relate in obvious or underlying ways to the present? Are there obvious or underlying resemblances between persons and/or situations in the text that give special meaning or provide insight for the present?

- What contemporary assumptions influence the way this passage is read, for good or for ill? What ideological issues are raised for modern readers by or over against the text?

- How representative is the congregation to those for whom the text was written originally? Is there an inherent disconnect that must be overcome in order to make the passage relevant?

- Would the original readers or hearers have been comforted/offended/challenged by this passage? What expectations would the readers have had each step of the way through the passage?

This approach is deliberately simple in form and does not require knowledge of original biblical languages. Preachers who are versed in established areas of biblical interpretation can do additional work to deepen their understanding of the text and connect it more closely with the context of the sermon.

Preachers should engage the texts critically before turning to commentaries; otherwise, the preacher does a disservice to her or his opportunity and ability to allow the text to speak to the specific context of preaching and to the preacher's own situation in proclaiming good news. The purpose of commentaries is to increase one's knowledge of the text and provide depth and support for one's own ideas. However, all would-be preachers should invest in an extensive and scholarly commentary of the Bible that gives careful attention to each book separately, in addition to an overview of the section of biblical writing in which it belongs, and that treats biblical periods, genres of biblical literature, themes, and history separately and with integrity. A good study Bible may also be helpful in providing simple background material that can give insight and assist in framing the text for preaching. My personal preference is *The New Interpreter's Bible: A Commentary in Twelve Volumes* (Nashville: Abingdon Press, 1994–1998) and *The New Interpreter's Study Bible: New Revised Standard Version with The Apocrypha* (Nashville: Abingdon Press, 2003); however, I believe it would be unethical to make specific suggestions for either a study Bible or Bible commentary. There are several academic and scholarly organizations that provide such information, and seminary librarians are generally also a good source. The checklist of questions provided in appendix B includes questions for both interpreting the text and connecting the text with the context of preaching. It may be used each time you do exegesis for an expository sermon or any biblical text.

A PROCESS FOR EXEGETING THE TOPICAL SERMON

Even a topical sermon finds its foundation in a biblical text, although the interpretation centers not so much in the meaning of one text, but in the application and meaning of the topic for the context of preaching. The foundational text on which the topic rests requires interpretation to connect it with the preaching context. Multiple texts may be used to support the topic, and an understanding of the role of each is necessary but does not require rigorous exegesis. The process outlined in this section and the list of questions provided in appendix C are suggestions only and are not to be considered prescriptive for topical exegesis. Please note the similarities in the processes of expository and topical exegesis.

1. Meet the topic
   - The purpose for addressing any topic is always to offer good news to the congregation.
   - The good news and the message arising from the topic together are intended to impact and support the discipleship of individuals and the congregation.

2. Establish the boundaries of the topic
   - Identify the wider, general topic that you intend to address. Break it apart into smaller, more manageable pieces and create an outline of topic and subtopics. For example, where faith is the general topic, the preacher may focus on the connection between prayer and faith or on the impact of faith on healing.
   - If this sermon is part of a series on a broader topic, verify that the flow of topics fits an appropriate pattern, or that subtopics are presented correctly to reach a desired goal.
   - If this is a stand-alone sermon, verify the purpose or goal of the sermon and the relevance of the topic to the situation of the congregation.

3. Narrow and frame the scope of the topic
   - Topical sermons are generally based on theology, Christian doctrine, or practice, which are open to broad interpretation biblically and theologically. For preaching, the scope of the topic moves from the general to the specific.
   - Using the outline of topic and subtopics created earlier in the process, select the specific topic for preaching.

- Develop a similar outline for the preaching topic (previously subtopic) that lists key points for preaching that exposes the topic to the congregation.
- Depending on the number of points, select three or four that may be presented in a sermon.

4. CONNECT THE TOPIC WITH THE BIBLE

- If the topic originated from a biblical text, exegete the text to verify the connection with the topic.
- Use the details/key points developed for the topic and the exegesis of the text to identify supporting texts.
- If the topic did not originate from scripture, use the key points that help to clarify the meaning of the topic to locate appropriate biblical texts that may provide the foundation for preaching the topic.
- Select and exegete a foundational text on which the topic of the sermon will rest.
- Exegete any secondary texts sufficiently to verify that they are representative of the meaning of the foundational text and of the preaching topic.

5. LOCATE THE TOPIC HISTORICALLY

- Consider and review the ways in which the topic has been approached historically and what scripture texts other preachers have used to address this topic.
- Investigate the way in which the topic and the texts used to support it have functioned in the church at large and in the present congregation.

6. SITUATE THE TEXT THEOLOGICALLY AND DOCTRINALLY

- Verify that the approach and the interpretation of the topic meets accepted theology.
- The subject of the topic must also be in accord with accepted Christian doctrines and with the denominational traditions of the congregation.

7. LOCATE THE TOPIC CONTEXTUALLY FOR PREACHING

- Locate the topic within the situation of the congregation. Restate the purpose for preaching on the particular topic.

- Check the relevance of the topic for the context of preaching and whether the message of the sermon fits the substance of the topic.

- If appropriate, consider the relevance of the topic to congregational, societal, or world issues.

In exegeting the topical sermon, avoid the temptation or the danger of using so much of the biblical material that the sermon becomes expository in content. The topical sermon is representative of a Christian doctrine or practice and the good news of the sermon leads to a call to discipleship within the context of that doctrine or practice but also supports the reality of divine grace. The checklist of questions provided in appendix C may be used each time you do exegesis for a topical sermon or any topic for preaching. It is a useful guide and not to be considered as the definitive method for exegeting a topic for preaching.

tHRee

■

Theological Constructs and Constraints
in Forming Good News Sermons

O n one of the first evenings of my Theology of Ministry I class in seminary, a visiting British minister, John Vincent,[1] shared his thoughts on theology for ministry. He said, "The best theologian for you is you." He clarified his words by explaining that only the individual can say exactly who or what God is for that person. Theology is defined as the study of God, and our theology speaks of our understanding of who God is for us individually and who or what God is for the world. The theological integrity of the sermon depends on the preacher's theology—how he or she understands God. How each of us experiences God is as different, as unique as our fingerprints. What we preach reveals our understanding of and relationship with God.

Fred Craddock, speaking of the situation of preaching, believes that each preacher needs to reassess not only one's role as a preacher but also "one's view of the congregation as the people of God, one's understanding of whether the sermon is the preacher's . . ."[2] In other words, while the theology of the preacher has a significant impact on the contents and the preaching of the sermon, it is preached in the midst of people, each of whom may have a different understanding of who God is in their life. The people may hold in common aspects of a particular theology, which also influences the development, contents, and preaching of the sermon.

This chapter considers the requirements for developing a good news sermon that is theologically sound and that is congruent with the gospel contained in scripture. It also addresses the question of how the preacher can be sure that the sermon offers a revelation of the God of scripture. While exegesis allows the preacher to look into, behind, and beneath the text to unearth its meaning for the present, the work of biblical interpretation does not uncover the full meaning of God or the Word of God for the life of the people. If the subject of the good news is God, and it is, then it follows that the preacher's understanding of God must include the conviction of grace as a key attribute of God. How does the preacher ensure that the sermon speaks clearly and accurately of the love of God? What safeguards can be put in place to help the preacher develop a sermon that is appropriate to the biblical record of the covenantal love of God? To do so requires that it be constructed with theological accuracy and integrity, particularly with respect to the truth of the love of God for all people.

"As a man thinketh in his heart so is he." That was my father's version of the Proverbs 23:7 text, and as he was wont to do, he used this biblical truism to express his displeasure when one of his children acted in objectionable ways. Applying that sentiment to the theology of the preacher I say: As the preacher believes about God in the heart, so that preacher preaches. A sermon cannot offer good news unless its message gives light to the majesty of God's love and unless it witnesses to the loving presence of God in human life and invites hearers to experience that love and offer their own witness to it through faithful discipleship. This chapter offers insights and exercises that will guide the preacher in developing good news sermons with theological integrity.

A THEOLOGY OF GOOD NEWS

Scripture, as the biblical record of God's interaction in the lives of human persons, is our chief accepted source of the good news. Scripture informs theology. It gives us ways to understand God, as creator, defender, protector, guide, liberator, and whatever attribute of God makes

God visible and available to you. Similarly, theology, the study of God and God's relationship to the created world and specifically the people of the world, informs our reading of scripture. Whatever our understanding of God, theology provides the lens through which we read the biblical record and interpret the stories of divine/human interaction recorded in the Bible. As preachers, we are inspired by the stories of the prophets from Moses through Elijah and Elisha, Isaiah and Jeremiah, Amos and Micah, and all the greater and lesser prophets who were mouthpieces for God. Their messages told of God's covenantal love for humanity, whether in affirmation or denouncement of the actions of the people. Through all the words of prophecy ran the thread of divine love that was never diminished by the burden of human sin and thus was always in reality a theology of good news.

A "theology of good news" keeps central the active and ongoing acceptance of God's grace that is above all and through all and in all things for the good of the whole people of God. A theology of good news speaks of God joyfully and invites hearers of the word into the fullness of joy that is the result of divine love. Theology is the source of the words of the good news sermon. There is a symbiotic relationship between theology and scripture. Each informs the other. How God is depicted in the stories of the Bible contributes to the development of one's theology. Often the bedrock of a preacher's theology is the uncritical childhood reading of scripture that defined the nature of God. Bible stories learned in early years often leave an indelible imprint that either hinders the preacher from accepting fully the attribute of grace that is the heart of God for created humanity or enables understanding. If the former, then the preacher may find it difficult to accept that all of scripture is founded on divine grace, that every text may be linked to the grace of God, and that the preacher has the opportunity to offer good news in every sermon.

Paul Scott Wilson also weighs in on the critical nature of good news as a missing element of many sermons. He offers several theological reasons for a change in the way that sermons are created.[3] He notes that the absence of God in our sermons may manifest that "God is missing from the center of our own lives."[4] Unless one's understanding of God includes one's personal experience of the same covenantal love that is the thread that runs through all of scripture, one is unable to witness to that truth with integrity. Even when the preacher understands and accepts the grace of God personally, that theological frame of reference does not appear explicitly when the preacher is not intentional in ensuring that the good news of the sermon is recognizable as such. The love of God created all things to be good; that love redeemed fallen humanity through Jesus Christ; and that same love unstintingly and unwaveringly guides and directs us through the Holy Spirit. Living in and preaching the great love of God comes from a theological understanding of God's transformative, regenerative love—a theology of good news that offers the hearers real good news.

This is a book on preaching and it does not represent a particular theology. One's theology shapes and is shaped by the preached Word of God, so having a theology of good news for preaching ensures that each sermon offers good news to the hearers. God's grace is active and ongoing, eternally creative and creating; shaping and reshaping fallen humanity into the image of Christ. This ongoing activity of redemption and salvation and the divine/human interaction it necessitates is the good news that brings overflowing life to those who accept and participate in it as a gift of grace. A preacher's theology of good news claims, articulates, and imparts to hearers the reality of the divine covenant.

The following questions will help you assess your own theology of good news:

1: DO YOU HAVE A CLEAR AND UNQUESTIONED UNDERSTANDING OF SCRIPTURE AS THE RECORD OF GOD'S COVENANTAL LOVE FOR HUMANITY?

Beyond the details of history and pseudohistory that comprise the biblical record is the Word of God. Theologically that means that inerrancy is not a prerequisite to the understanding of the real presence of God in history and specifically in the record of those whose lives have been chronicled for posterity. The Judeo-Christian heritage that has been embraced by the church gives substance to divine love that is often misunderstood, misrepresented, and unfathomable. That love portrayed in scripture is the fulfillment of covenant, made and kept by God, accepted and broken across time by human beings. And it is the biblical witness of that unbroken covenant that leaps from the pages of antiquity and that the preacher must embrace and engage in order to give voice to the good news that it offers. Although the scripture text may lend itself to good news preaching, the authentic witness of scripture comes not from simply preaching the words, but from the preacher's application of her or his theological stance, one that is directed and supported by the preacher's belief in the good news of divine grace.

In studying scripture, the preacher must look beyond the immediacy of translated words, and retold and reframed stories, to recognize, understand, and witness to the presence and work of God in the situations of the biblical stories. This requires an act of faith. By faith the preacher is moved to accept the unfathomable and to believe the unexplainable as it applies to the love of God for all people. The words of scripture retold by preachers and by the church may even offer contradictions in the record of events and places and people. It is nevertheless the Word of God, "useful for teaching, for reproof, for correction, and for training in righteousness" (2 Tim. 3:16), and these activities are all requisite to the shaping of one's theology. Accepting the biblical record with the caveat of divine inspiration requires an act of faith.

While scripture may not engender faith, accepting scripture by faith enables the preacher to see more clearly the presence of God in scripture and to give credence appropriately to the messages of God's love that are woven into the texts of scripture. By faith the preacher stands not simply to relate the stories of old, but through these timeworn yet timeless stories to call the people and to join with them in becoming active participants in the divine/human drama that witnesses to the grace of God. Scripture is thus a sustaining word for the preacher who is empowered to share that faith in the good news offered through the sermon.

2: DO YOU EXPERIENCE A SENSE OF JOY WHEN YOU SEE THE EVIDENCE OF GOD'S GRACE IN THE BIBLE?

Many preachers feel a sense of compulsion to call hearers to live fully into their Christian identity, but too many in their disciple-making zeal have resorted to harangue and threats as the way of salvation.

Congregations have been beaten up and knocked down by preachers who are filled with a sense of doom because of the state of humanity and the world at large. When that is the worry in the preacher's heart, it is impossible to be joyful or to encourage hearers to experience the joy of God's presence even in the midst of the world's greatest disasters. In other words, not only is there no good news, but the preacher is lost in a morass of death and destruction and has missed the celebration of the overcoming wrought by God's enlivening presence.

Certainly there are scripture texts that seem to speak of anything but love, joy, and peace, the attributes normally associated with the grace of God. But with careful and authentic interpretation of biblical texts in their historical contexts, one may find the not-so-hidden love of God beneath their obvious and often distressing representation in the record of scripture. The preacher that takes the biblical text only at face value may lose sight of its true meaning in the historical context and use the text inappropriately. What may appear as God's unrepentant anger at the people's fickleness may hide the loving concern that underlies God's severe response to the people's actions.

Similarly the preacher who looks at the present situation and compares it to the biblical record that depicts the punishment of an angry God is inclined to miss the moments of divine grace that are interwoven in the text and that served to bring the people back into right relationship with God and with each other. But the preacher who is driven by a theology of good news will search beneath the words of the text to discover the treasure trove of God's love that is ever present in divine actions. Such a discovery calls forth joyful praise and thanksgiving for the inestimable love of God.

3: IS YOUR RELATIONSHIP WITH SCRIPTURE IN DEVELOPING THE SERMON AN AFFIRMING EXPERIENCE?

The work of developing the sermon for preaching invites the preacher to experience and invest in a sincere and serious relationship with God, with the people of God, and with scripture, the Word of God. The preacher's relationship with the words of scripture helps to increase the knowledge and understanding of the presence of God and ultimately informs and shapes the preacher's theology in a systematic way. Studying the biblical stories sharpens knowledge and increases wisdom about what it means to be constant recipients of the grace of God. Thus the text shapes the preacher's theology, and the systemization of the preacher's theology influences how the preacher proclaims the good news.

The preacher's experience with scripture, specifically for developing the sermon, not only involves delving into the words and the underlying meaning of scripture texts but requires also that the preacher maintain communication with God throughout the process to ensure that the words of the sermon represent the Word of God for the people. The preacher's ongoing conversation with God as it pertains to scripture must be for the purpose of discerning the Word of God that arises from the particular text, for the specific event of preaching. How the preacher experiences this influences the way in which the preacher approaches scripture as the repository of good news.

Each event of preaching offers an opportunity to search or wrestle with the scripture text for the good news that it contains. The good news preacher approaches the text with the expectation of finding good news, and when that venture meets with success it affirms both the divine/human dialogue of prayer and the faith that caused the preacher to undertake the search in the first place. The preacher thus becomes a witness to scripture as a record of God's love for humanity and celebrates the success through the words of the sermon and by subsequent forays into the Bible for the purpose of finding and preaching good news.

BIBLICAL THEOLOGY: FINDING GRACE

Paul Scott Wilson, in his contribution to the *Festschrift* in honor of David Buttrick, notes Buttrick's concern with the influence of biblical theology on homiletics. Both homileticians considered the distance between the Bible and the present to be detrimental to the preaching task, and one particular area of their concern is the ability of the preacher to interpret the biblical text appropriately for hearers in the present. As Wilson named it, in order to reconnect the Bible and preaching, "the focus must be on helping preachers to move from the biblical text to the contemporary situation and on recasting theology in the present."[5]

Biblical theology not only sheds light on the meaning of the text, it re-veals God's initiating, creating presence; frames the need for and the substance of God's redemption as the offset to human sin; and gives substance to the sustaining presence of God in human endeavor that originates from the heart of divine love. It is the Word of God for the people of God that calls forth a doxological response from people and preacher together.

Biblical theology digs into the historical record of God contained in scripture to identify how believers understand who God is. There is no single doctrinal position that is central or uniform with respect to bib-lical theology. In fact, the very resources that have been engaged in the effort to make the meaning of scripture clearer and more accessible for preaching have often run counter to the need of homiletics that "seeks to render the Word of God in a manner that is faithful to the biblical witness, scholarship, and tradition, yet is specific to our time."[6] In that sense, the preacher undertakes the task of biblical theology in order to help to connect text and context so that the claims of the sermon are in accord with the claims of the scripture text on which it stands. Biblical interpretation meets theological understanding as the substance of bib-lical theology for preaching.

Good news preaching offers grace from each text. Biblical theology reveals the grace that resides in the text. The following questions may help unearth that grace in the text:

WHAT DOES THE TEXT SAY ABOUT GOD OR THE ACTION OF GOD?

Since a significant portion of the biblical record does not speak openly of God's love in action, it requires an interpretive process to unearth God's activity of grace or even God's presence in the context of histor-ical events. It is important that the preacher not rush to name God as principal when the action seems to give evidence of the mark of the di-vine. An example of such misrepresentation may be seen in the parables, where God is often assigned the role of master or king as in the parable of the wicked tenants, or as father as in the parable of the prodigal son. The preacher's investigation into the historical realities surrounding the text, whether as a lived reality or by the influence on persons who are one step removed from the events, must be carefully deconstructed to authentically unearth the divine action. The purpose of that task is to verify that the preacher's theological conclusions are both accurate and appropriate.

DOES THE CLAIM OF DIVINE GRACE ARISE FROM THE CONTENTS OF THE BIBLICAL TEXT?

The unbroken thread throughout all of scripture is covenant. God makes and keeps covenant with humanity. Human beings make or agree to a covenantal relationship with God and constantly and consistently break the covenant. Divine grace operates within that covenant and speaks more clearly about divine love than about human desire. Thus in determining the claim of grace, the preacher must consider carefully the true meaning of the text and decipher its contribution to the people's understanding and acceptance of the unbounded love of God. The language of scripture must flow into the present in a way that enables the Word of God to be recognized in the language of the people of faith.

· · ·

The preacher's theology is shaped not only by scripture, but also by the church and by society at large. Over the centuries of its existence the church has worked deliberately to define its theology. Differences based on the understanding of scripture have resulted in differing doctrines and denominational splits, which may well have a direct influence not only on the reading and understanding of scripture, but also on the preacher's understanding of the divine/human relationship. A theology of good news for all people, which Jesus declared as his mission, helps the preacher to avoid the trap of categorizing the hearers either as the chosen of God and exclusive recipients of God's favor, or the condemned who are beyond the grace of God.

The community, subject to the particular theology of their denomination, may resist hearing the good news of unfettered grace for all people, but the preacher must, in turn, resist the seductive pull of being among the chosen and allow the witness of scripture to stand as proof to the nature of the grace of God given freely to all people. Likewise, faced with a text of scripture that seems to discriminate and therefore segregate humanity into selective groups, the preacher is challenged to resist the temptation to speak so narrowly to the present congregation that the words of the sermon take the hearers outside of the beloved community. Every sermon must offer good news that is authentic to the eternal covenant that defines the love of God for the whole of humanity.

Good news preaching requires language that works as a filter between the words of scripture and the unrelenting cries of the people. Symbols of the Christian faith such as creation, sin, redemption, new birth, the community in Christ, and eternal life are encompassed in the good news sermon because they are the core of scripture, the essence of the divine/human relationship, and the reality of God's covenant of love in action in the lives of individuals and the community. The preacher cannot dismiss one in preference to the other, because they all represent the core of Christianity and therefore of Christian preaching.

Theological adequacy and appropriateness are the mandate of every preacher and every sermon. However neither requirement can be met fully unless the sermon intentionally and specifically offers good news. In the midst of tragedy and persecution the ancient writers worked diligently to show that God was present with the people. In times of slavery and exile, of disobedience and unfaithfulness, in persecution and oppression, God was present. That was the message of the prophets and the temple, of synagogue and church worshipers, who all listened for the Word of God from the preachers of their time.

The people of God in this time are still seeking and expecting an authentic word of divine grace from the mouth of today's preachers. The Bible is still the trusted record of divine love in history, and the preacher who stands to declare a message to the church in the name of God does so wisely with awesome fear and through divine grace. Each preacher is constrained in preaching by this reality, but is also empowered to construct a sermon that not only speaks of the historical reality of the love of God, but that offers it freely to the present congregation through the words of the sermon. The contents of the sermon, developed from the preacher's theology, are thus proclaimed as testimonial to the active, empowering love of God. And that is good news preaching.

four

■

Connecting and Contextualizing
the Good News Sermon
for Your Congregation

very sermon is contextual. Sermons are preached to a particular people, at a particular time and place. Preaching that is not contextual creates a void between preacher and people. My personal experience of this occurred when I used an illustration from a popular song by Janet Jackson, an African American pop artist, in a sermon preached to my white upper-middle-class congregation. The illustration was right on target with the content of my sermon but it missed the mark completely in this community. Contextualizing the sermon requires knowing the social, cultural, theological, and doctrinal norms as well as the experiences of the community past and present. Without this knowledge the gap between preacher and people, sermon and good news becomes an ever-widening chasm as the preacher continues preaching above, below, or beyond the people or in a way that is unconcerned or unconnected with their lives.

In this chapter we look at the nature of preaching as contextual and the reason, purpose, and importance of contextualization in preaching. We consider some simple tools that facilitate the creation of sermons that are contextualized to fit and therefore connect with the congregations to whom they are preached. My particular focus is the development of good news that is appropriate to the context of preaching. Preachers are helped in their preaching when they take time to learn about the people to whom they preach. The preacher who arrives in a congregation with the feeling that he or she knows exactly what the people need to hear, and who takes no time to meet and greet the people before preaching to them about their need for better discipleship, does a disservice to the people, to the text, to him- or herself, and to God. Especially in such situations, otherwise good sermons fall flat because a sermon is effective only when it connects with the people. The preached news is not good if it does not reach the people with an appropriate message of God's grace.

CONTEXTUAL GOOD NEWS PREACHING

Contextual preaching allows the content of the sermon to be in accordance with the culture and needs of the congregation. However, at times good news that speaks of grace for all people, including those beyond the congregation, may not initially be considered good news by the hearers of the sermon. A good example of this is a church that has shut its doors and retreated behind those doors because of new people in the community. The preacher who comes to this congregation, learns the culture of separatism, and preaches within those boundaries is neither preaching contextually nor offering good news. On the other hand, if the preacher contextualizes the sermon, it could offer divine grace as a means of addressing and overcoming the fear or other emotions that have caused the prevailing attitude. In doing so, not only does the sermon take account of the congregation's cultural context, but it also offers real good news. In this way the content of good news arises out of the text, and it connects with and addresses the congregation's situation. With these elements meeting together, the sermon earns the title of a contextual good news sermon.

Good news preaching intentionally, appropriately, and explicitly offers the good news of divine grace to the gathered community in a particular time and place. This definition emphasizes both the preacher's responsibility to proclaim good news that is the purpose of every sermon, and the requirement to be intentional in ensuring that the sermon is appropriate to the hearers. Contextualizing the sermon requires that one engage a process of congregational analysis that is concurrent with the work of biblical interpretation. The pastor/preacher who lives with the people on a daily basis must be as intentional about analyzing the congregation for preaching as does the visiting preacher. Life is never static, and, although the yesterdays help to inform the present-day moment of preaching, the preacher does well to keep in step with the changes in society, the culture, and the world as well as in the congregation itself, as all these affect the content and shape of the congregation.

Just as the congregation changes physically over time, so too does it change theologically because of the same influences of culture, church, and world that affect the preacher. The congregation's experiences of God-with-us give substance and credibility to their faith and directly affect the theological belief and structure of the church. The preacher who is concerned with the issue of contextualization also recognizes that although there may be a predominant theological position in the congregation, there are generally many theologies that are subordinate to the corporate theology of the group but that are just as influential in shaping the theological context of the community.

Whether it is the substance of the gospel itself, the preacher's struggle with the revelation of the good news, or the ability of the congregation to hear the good news of the sermon, by the preacher's contextualizing the sermon, the good news has a greater chance of reaching the hearers. The contents of scripture and the salvific message of the gospel are often as challenging for Christians as for non-Christians. At times preachers struggle with their own faith as they try to experience the revelation of the Word of God that is present in the text and appropriate for the context of preaching. However, on every occasion of preaching, the preacher faces the challenge of hearing the good news of the text, of developing a sermon that is inviting to the hearers and then of delivering the sermon in a way that captures and holds the attention of the hearers.

In order to meet these challenges, the preacher maintains communication with God and takes direction from the Holy Spirit, but contextualizing the sermon to fit the occasion of preaching and the congregation to whom it will be preached helps in addressing the issue and even in overcoming the challenge of ensuring that the message of good news reaches the hearers. Ultimately the work of preaching and the revelation of the Word of God is the work of the Holy Spirit. It is God who initiates the action of revelation. It is God who in self-revelation joins with the spoken words of proclamation, and this occurs in the context of the church, the gathered body of Christ. This is how preaching becomes an act of revelation of the good news of the mitigating grace of God for humanity. Contextualizing the words of the sermon means going beyond the context of the worship experience in which preaching takes place, and where the preacher and the hearers are located, to the wider context of the culture in which the hearers live their everyday lives. In this way the people experience a new hearing at every event of preaching even when the text is familiar or even well known to the congregation. Contextual preaching allows the congregation to hear, and perhaps even to see, what God has done and is doing in their world. It addresses the reality of the congregation's situation, and in the proclamation of the good news of God's redemptive work the distance of history is overcome and God is made visible and audible to the people in that time and place.

CONTEXTUALIZATION AS HOMILETICAL CONVERSATION

Within the congregation there are formal and informal groups that share history, are connected by familial ties, that have cherished friendships, or are separated by tensions of life and living in community. The conversations within these groupings give substance to the understandings of self, church, community, and the presence of God as active in the many iterations of life. Because these conversations embody and direct how the congregation is constructed, the preacher does well to pay careful attention to them and to the nonverbal interactions of the community. In many instances the preacher is not an active member of these conversational groups, nor may the preacher be actively aware of the ongoing conversations.

O. Wesley Allen describes the church as a community engaged in ongoing "circles of conversation in which church talk seriously engages all of the other conversations going on in our culture [and] members of the congregation are seen not only as recipients of the church's proclamation but also providers of it."[1] The differing theologies of individuals are often brought to light in the conversational circles that are representative of the beliefs and allegiances of the members of the congregation. The savvy pastor/preacher will be intentional about honing in on these conversations and bringing to light the theologies that are present and operating in the congregation as an initial step to the pastoral task and, by extension, the preaching responsibility. The singular purpose in undertaking this often time-consuming activity is to present the good news appropriately.

Contextualization makes preaching communal, and the conversations of the community are significant for preaching contextually. Through contextualization preacher and people become equal owners of the sermon, and this allows the good news of the sermon to relate equally to both preacher and hearers. The sermon represents ongoing dialogue between three sets of partners—God and the preacher, God and the people, and the preacher and the people. In each case it is true dialogue, a conversation in which the two parties both speak and listen. The preaching event, when it is effective, is representative of the intersection of the three separate yet related conversations.

1. God and the preacher—The preacher's conversation with God through prayer and scripture provides direction for the selection of the good news and the contents of the sermon. Active, daily communication with God enables the preacher to identify the divine voice in the midst of the competing voices of the world.

2. God and the people—God speaks to all people, and in the case of the sermon, God speaks to the hearers to prepare them to receive the Word. The hearers also speak to God asking for a word for their lives, and God is present in the various conversations that take place at the many levels that operate among the people of God.

3. The preacher and the people—This conversation facilitates the preacher's knowledge of what the people expect from the sermon and thus helps to direct the preacher's response to the needs of the

people. It also helps to verify the accuracy of the preacher's under-standing of the conversation with God that determined the con-tents of the sermon.

The conversations that are part of the communal life of the congrega-tion are essential to the preacher's work of contextualizing the sermon. They also affect the way that we hear and receive the good news of the sermon and help to advance the people of God in their discipleship. These homiletical conversations are essential for the discernment of the gospel message that is offered to address the needs of the people in the particular time and place of each preaching event.

The visiting preacher who cannot be a part of the congregational conversations can nevertheless be part of an ongoing dialogue engaged by the whole people of God. The substance of this conversation is fo-cused on the church and its place and mission in the world. The good news of the presence of God in all of life and in empowering the whole people of God for ministry in the name of Jesus Christ is part and par-cel of this dialogue and allows the preacher who does not have access to the specific congregational context to preach in a way that fits the church as the body of Christ.

CONTEXTUALIZING THE GOOD NEWS SERMON

Contextualizing the good news of Jesus Christ in a way that inspires the people as Christian disciples is the ongoing task of the pastor/preacher as a spiritual leader of the church. It is the substance of the church's life and the goal of practical ministry. It is the mission of the church, and it affects the hearers as individuals, it affects the commu-nity gathered for the worship of Christ, and ultimately it affects the whole world. When the people receive the good news in a way that touches their lives, they are transformed and they in turn become agents of Christ for the transformation of the world. But whether or not the preacher is also the pastor of the congregation where he or she is preaching, developing and preaching the sermon in a way that makes the good news resonate with the hearers is essential at every moment of preaching.

Contextualizing the good news sermon means shaping the good news in language that is familiar so that the people who hear it can recognize and claim its place in their lives. It means making concrete the Christian message of God's saving grace by applying it directly to the substance of people's everyday lives and offering specific ways in which hearers can be transformed by God's grace to become better disciples of Jesus Christ. It means using language that hearers not only understand but that is meaningful to their lives, that touches them in familiar ways so that they do not need to define the words or interpret their meaning to lay claim to the message. It does not mean being simplistic, but it does mean making the message sufficiently simple that the hearers are not forced to define each word in order for it to make sense to their ears and in their lives.

In addition, contextualizing the good news means recognizing the communal nature of the congregation and allowing the message of good news to impact the corporate life of the church even as it affects each individual personally as disciples of Jesus Christ. Although the preacher preaches one sermon, and each hearer receives the message in the way that makes the offering of good news appropriate to her/his life, true contextualization also considers the community as a body—the body of Christ. The good news of divine love for humanity does not change, and is never exhausted, but placed within the context of the gathered community, it re-forms the people individually and then out of their individualities into one body, under one head, Jesus Christ. In this way the community takes shape and assumes its identity as the body of Christ. Good news preaching keeps present the reality of both the individual and the community under their shared identity in Christ. The good news of the sermon offers the assurance that God is present and at work in the lives of individuals, in the community, and in the world. Contextualizing the good news sermon requires that it must be connected not only to the individuals and the gathered community, but also to the mission of Christ in the world. Contextualizing the good news sermon allows the preacher to help the community accept the good news of the gospel as the force for shaping their lives in Christ and for carrying out the mission of Christ in the world.

"TOOLS" FOR CONTEXTUALIZING THE GOOD NEWS SERMON

The tools for preaching exist mainly within the preacher. Although there are methods of creating and preaching the sermon that may be learned, generally the implements required for creating and delivering the sermon lie within the mind and heart of the preacher. Similarly the tools for contextualizing the good news sermon, when learned, become part of the preacher and part of the natural process of shaping the sermon for presenting good news. The three "tools" necessary to the creation and delivery of contextualized good news sermons are as follows:

A theology of good news: This prepares the preacher to approach the text with expectation and anticipation of finding good news in, behind, beneath, or around the text. A theology of good news gives the assurance that God is always working for the ultimate good of the people of God. It directs the investigation into each text from the position of anticipation of unearthing the evidence of divine grace. It prepares the preacher for the celebration that accompanies the realization of God's active, transforming, empowering presence in human endeavors.

Knowledge of the context: Whether pastor or visitor, the preacher must expend the effort that is required to understand the situation of preaching. Knowing the social, cultural, theological, spiritual, and political culture of the people as well as the specific situation of the preaching moment, such as the denominational and liturgical contexts, enables the preacher to develop the sermon in a way that speaks to the reality of the hearers' situation and also to discern corporate needs that can shape the offering of the good news for the congregation.

The assurance of grace: The preacher who has an ongoing relationship with God gives witness to the presence of God in the activities of humanity. However, the assurance of divine presence must encompass the belief that God's presence is one of grace. Frank Thomas expounds on the idea of celebration in preaching, which he says comes from "the assurance of grace,"[2] and preaching as part of the liturgy of the church provides a natural place of celebration and a venue for delivering the good news. The preacher must live in the assurance of God's grace actively working for the good of humanity in order to develop and deliver good news sermons into the context of the lives of the people of God.

• • •

Framing the contents of the sermon and the good news appropriately for the congregation is the ongoing task of every preacher. Every sermon is preached into a particular context—of time, place, and people. Even the Word of God whispered into our hearts and minds is contextual. "God's word does not ignore us and our circumstances, speaking imperiously as if none of that mattered."[3] And neither should the preacher. All preaching is contextual, whether or not the preacher designs the sermon with the specific situation in mind. But in order for the good news to reach the hearers in a way that makes it transformative for their lives, it requires full preparedness of self and spirit on the part of the preacher. The preacher prepares to receive good news long before the preparation of the sermon begins or the moment of preaching is engaged.

THE HOLY SPIRIT IN THE WORK OF CONTEXTUALIZATION

Good news preaching requires that the good news of the sermon is contextualized first for the preacher and through the preacher in the power of the Holy Spirit, for the people. Only in this way can the preacher hope to connect spiritually with the congregation. Even when the preacher has an ecclesiastical relationship with the congregation, it is impossible to bring the good news alive to the congregation, to connect spiritually with the people, unless it is through the power of the Holy Spirit. The Holy Spirit orders the life of the church, and the preacher must tap into that source in order to preach authentic good news to the people of God.

The Holy Spirit is the giver of all gifts that enable the work of the church. The recipients of such gifts are charged in their use "to equip the saints for the work of ministry, for building up the body of Christ" (Eph. 4:12). In the same way that the preacher's life and ministry is a gift of the Holy Spirit, so too is the specific task of developing the sermon for preaching and for contextualizing the good news of the sermon for the hearers. The preacher who approaches the task without seeking direction from God, and who offers the sermon without the guidance of the Holy Spirit, creates a situation that may result in the message either being rejected or not being heard. However, because the Holy Spirit directs the whole work of the church, the hearers may yet receive good news even in the face of the preacher's omission. Ultimately, good news preaching is effective in its context not simply because of the work of the preacher, but through the preacher by the power of the Holy Spirit. Preacher and people thus experience the good news of divine grace, proclaimed in the words of the sermon and taking effect in the lives of the whole people of God, through the power and presence of the Holy Spirit.

five

■

Shaping Sermons to Effectively Present Good News

his chapter offers a weekly process for developing a good news sermon. I developed and used this process during my many years as a pastor in a local congregation. I invariably followed the *Revised Common Lectionary* for preaching, and since most of my sermons were expository, the proposed process is directly applicable to that style of sermon. It may be adapted, however, for developing topical sermons, because scripture provides the foundation for all sermons.

To that end I have included some suggestions for developing a topical sermon. The process calls for developing the sermon over six days of the week, starting on Monday. If your weekly service of worship occurs on a day other than Sunday, adjust the starting day to the day following the worship service. By spreading the work over six days, you have more time, in the midst of the busy schedule of pastoral duties, to give appropriate attention to the text and to the context of preaching; the material is more likely to be impacted by the context, and you have more time to listen for the internal and external messages that give light and meaning to the text. Further, including your work of developing the sermon as part of your larger weekly schedule within the congregation will allow you to set aside the time you need to prepare well.

If you prefer to do your sermons weeks or months in advance, the process can still be used to spread out the activities over a number of days, but be sure to review the sermon two or three days before preaching it to check that it is still contextual for the hearers. The amount of time you have available for sermon preparation depends of course on your schedule, and congregational responsibilities may dictate the days of the week that are most favorable to the work of sermon development, but it is important that the work not be relegated to one day. The process assumes that the preacher reads and studies scripture on a regular basis and is not dependent on the limited time available on a weekly basis to do all the work of interpreting the biblical texts. As interpretive work is done, or as the preacher increases his or her knowledge of scripture and theological understanding, he or she should maintain the material in a way that keeps it available for use in preparing future sermons.

The process assumes also that the preacher has taken or is taking the time to become familiar with the context of the preaching event, whether or not the sermon is intended for a regular weekly worship service and the preacher is also the pastor of the congregation. Further, the process assumes that the preacher has daily devotional time that includes prayer and the reading of scripture and perhaps meditation. I suggest that the preacher use part of this devotional time or perhaps extend the length of devotional time on some days for developing the sermon. In any event, throughout the process of sermon development, saturate your work in prayer. The Holy Spirit empowers the preacher in both developing and preaching of the sermon. A schedule that summarizes this process is provided in Appendix D.

This chapter also presents a general outline that may be used for shaping a sermon, describes several common styles of sermon, and shows how to create detailed outlines for several different styles of sermon. The exercise of creating sermon outlines uses the same text to demonstrate how to present the good news garnered from the text and allow it to function as the nucleus around which to develop the good news sermon, regardless of the sermonic style selected for preaching.

A WEEKLY PROCESS FOR SERMON DEVELOPMENT

MONDAY: READ THE TEXT

If you have selected a scripture text for preaching, read it as part of your morning devotions and listen prayerfully to the text to hear the specific good news that it offers to the preaching context. If you follow the lectionary for preaching and have not yet selected your text for preaching, read all the scripture passages and listen for the one that resonates spiritually with you, as preacher, and contextually with the situation of the congregation as you understand it. Use lectionary-based devotional material to give you further insights into the text. Read the full pericope and listen carefully for the message of divine grace that arises from the text. The text may suggest a style of sermon—expository or topical; however, if you have already determined to preach a topical sermon, consider the appropriateness of the topic to the text. If time permits, read more than one translation of the text.

TUESDAY: READ AND EXEGETE THE TEXT

Again in the interest of time, read the text as part of your morning devotions, but schedule additional time to begin the work of interpretation. The work on this second day of the sermon development process focuses on the interpretation of the text or topic and the identification of the good news and the creation of the discipleship message that will drive the sermon. A helpful exercise for this purpose is described in chapter 2, which identifies the good news and the message to be preached by determining the *what, so what?* and *now what?* of the sermon.

This initial work of interpretation or exegesis involves research and data gathering. In the same way that reading the text brings to the fore ideas that give special meaning to the week's events and conversations and vice versa, the background data you gather during the research of the text or topic also becomes a lens through which to see and experience the events of the day or the week. As a result, otherwise unimportant actions, tasks, or happenings take on new meaning when observed or experienced through the frame of reference of both the text and its background. These dual filters are helpful in contextualizing the sermon.

This interpretive work of exegesis also requires reflection in order to select what is important to include in the sermon. Good research may unearth significant data that illumines the text; however, such study exegesis is often not appropriate sermon exegesis. I suggest that you make it a practice to access many types of resources for biblical interpretation, including paper and electronic texts and images, and it can be helpful to print out background material if it cannot be easily bookmarked and accessed during sermon writing. Whatever research method you use, and whether or not you use a manuscript for preaching, proper biblical interpretation is a necessity for developing a sermon that offers good news to the hearers.

In every case, whatever the format, the exegesis of the text is necessary for connecting the text with the context and for appropriating the good news of the text for the hearers.

WEDNESDAY: FRAME THE SERMON

In many churches this midweek day is also the day for adult Bible study led by the pastor, and it can be a difficult day in which to carve out time for sermon development. On the other hand, depending on the schedule of weekly church events, this may be the best day for creating the sermon manuscript. If so, expect to devote a significant part of the day to the task. By this time of the week you should have most, if not all, of the exegetical work completed and should have a clear idea of the good news you want to share, the message you want to deliver, and the general contents of the sermon, including stories, images, or illustrations you plan to include. Completing the interpretive activities as early as possible in the week allows you time to consider the shape and contents of the sermon. It also leaves you time to shape the sermon in a way that will attract and hold the attention of the hearers.

Whether or not you create a full sermon manuscript, complete any remaining exegetical work today and if you will use an outline, develop one based on the style or shape of the sermon you have selected. The outline is the frame within which the substance of the sermon will be housed, and which diagrams the movement that takes the sermon to its planned conclusion. If you choose to create one, the outline of the sermon should be as detailed as is necessary to flesh out the ideas, and as structured as is required to show the flow of the movement of the material being presented to the hearers. Include the intended contents of each part of the sermon and the image or illustrations to be used to give substance to the message. Examples of sermon outlines for several different styles of sermons are included later in this chapter.

If you develop an outline, give as careful attention to the introduction and conclusion as you do to shaping the body of the sermon. The more careful and detailed the outline, the easier it will be to review the appropriateness of the contents of the sermon once the manuscript is produced. Often the intended contents or the planned conclusion may dictate a particular sermonic form, or you may select a style of sermon and develop the outline to make the contents fit that shape. In any event you are well served to plan as much of the material to be included in the sermon as possible before actually creating the full-blown manuscript. If you typically preach without a manuscript, this may be the outline you use as pulpit notes when you preach the sermon.

THURSDAY: PREPARE THE SERMON MANUSCRIPT

If you have not done so already, create the sermon manuscript, and I do highly recommend you create a full manuscript for all sermons. I have heard many preachers who protest the need for a sermon manuscript and profess their ability to preach well without first producing the sermon in written form. While this is true of many gifted preachers, most of the sermons from the many not-so-gifted preachers, who deny the need to prepare a manuscript and claim their ability to preach effectively without such preparation, except in rare cases do not live up to the advanced billing. Congregations are plagued by preachers who ramble, lose their place, introduce unnecessary and sometimes erroneous material, leave stories hanging, or otherwise fail at the task of preaching a cohesive, comprehensive, and effective sermon.

Creating a manuscript does not mean you have to preach from the manuscript, but a manuscript does help organize the sermonic material in an ordered fashion. It helps to give substance to the ideas that surface in your mind, yet still allows you to review and reshape those ideas for effective presentation. It also helps to ensure that the exegetical material included is appropriate. The good news and message statements and the sermon outline already developed help to simplify the task. Once the manuscript is drafted, I recommend that you walk away and allow the material of the sermon to permeate your mind and the heart. If you have done your job well, then the exegetical material, the good news statement, the message statement, and the sermon outline together will enable you to create a strong sermon manuscript.

FRIDAY: READ, REVIEW, REVISE, REFORMULATE

Read and review your manuscript prayerfully and carefully. Reviewing the contents considers both text and context. Whether the sermon is expository or topical, and in whatever style it is created, its contents must appropriately connect the biblical foundation with the present situation and needs of the people. In reviewing the manuscript, begin by comparing it against the outline. Is the movement from one section to the next clear and smooth? Do the transitions between sections make sense? If not, prune until they are. Pruning will always help to sharpen your sermon contents, even if it's painful at the time. Review the contents by reading the sermon aloud so that you can experience the sermon through multiple senses—sight, speech, and hearing. Reading the sermon aloud helps you to check the appropriateness of the language, and whether the sermon delivers on its promise of good news and therefore can be heard—well.

Learn to listen self-critically to all aspects of your sermon as you read it through. Verify that the contents are appropriate to the shape—for example, the contents of the pages in the Four Pages of the Sermon model, the progression from exegesis to theological exposition to application in the Puritan Plain style, the movement of points or tasks to the intended message of good news and the call to discipleship. Verifying the shape helps to ensure that the sermon is designed in the way that facilitates the offering of good news. As for content, review your use of exegetical material, imagery, and illustrations, and verify that the sermon makes sense, that it offers a message of discipleship, and, above all, that it clearly offers good news.

Most of the time you will need to make revisions to the draft manuscript—sometimes quite substantial ones, and, if the sermon obviously isn't working, have the courage to start over. Once you have made revisions, practice reading the sermon aloud, preferably in front of a mirror. This way you actually *hear* the words or ideas that aren't quite clear or cause you to stumble. If you opt not to preach with a manuscript, be sure you memorize enough of the sermon, and especially the outline and the structure, really well. Resist memorizing the entire sermon, however, as that may make the delivery sound too canned. The sermon would thus lack spontaneity and might hinder both its hearing and the preacher's connection with the congregation.

If you do not preach from a full manuscript and use an outline or a set of notes, this is also the day to practice using the outline or the notes by attempting to preach a full sermon. Become as familiar as possible with the contents of your sermon. The more prepared you are, the better will be your delivery of the sermon. The more familiar you are with the material of your sermon, the more freedom you have to connect with the congregation when you preach it. The freedom you gain from practicing also gives you more opportunity to experience the presence of the Holy Spirit in your delivery of the sermon.

SATURDAY: REREAD THE SERMON, ABSORB THE MESSAGE, AND RELAX

Whether this is a day of limited parish activity that allows time for relaxation, or if, as in my experience in one parish, it is a day of frenetic activity, try to relax from the work of creating the sermon. You may choose to read the complete sermon as part of the day's devotion or set aside a special time in which to review it.

The hope is that by today you are making only minimal changes to the sermon and you can focus on becoming more familiar with its contents. By this sixth day it is too late to begin writing a sermon or even to make major revisions to a written sermon. Instead of trying to make the sermon a work of perfection, use whatever time you have to become more at ease with your written material.

Other than that, relax! Allow the message to settle deep into your mind and spirit with the assurance that the Holy Spirit will complete the work of preaching by making your sermon take effect in the lives of the hearers.

SUNDAY: PREACH THE SERMON AND LET IT GO

This is the moment for which you have been preparing throughout the week. If time permits, as part of your personal morning devotion, reread the sermon so that it is fixed clearly in your mind and heart. Resist changing it at this point because that will only confuse you. Trust that you have done what you can, and leave the rest up to God—unless of course you notice an egregious mistake, or unless something disastrous has happened in the congregation, in society, or in the world that makes the message of the sermon completely inappropriate. A good example of this is my experience of being called to the bedside of the church organist, who died unexpectedly in my presence very early on the Sunday morning in December that was scheduled as the church's Christmas celebration. Once I arrived at the worship service I was compelled to change much of both the liturgy and the sermon to allow the church to hear and respond appropriately to the news of the death of a beloved servant of God.

Failing such extraordinary situations, having been conscientious and faithful to the text and to the process of sermon development, you can rest easy knowing that the good news and the message of discipleship that you have put together in the sermon are appropriate to both text and context. All that is left is for you to trust in divine grace and go forward to offer good news to the people of God. Trust that God will allow the message to reach the hearts of those who need to hear it, and relax so that there is also space in your mind and heart for the Holy Spirit to work within you, the preacher.

• • •

Although this weekly process has served me well over many years of preaching as pastor in a local congregation, there are many similar models that may work just as well. The important thing is to have a process that is measured and focused over several days. Attempting to do all the work of developing the sermon in one day and at the last minute is foolhardy. More often than not the minimal effort will fail to produce a worthy sermon and your preaching will be an affront to both the people and to God. As I tell my students, prepare, prepare, prepare! Give the Holy Spirit something to work with!

FRAMING THE OUTLINE OF THE SERMON

Each sermon has three basic and discrete sections:

1. *Introduction:* This should capture the attention of the congregation by meeting them where they are and point the direction in which the sermon will move.

2. *Body:* This contains the substance of the sermon and makes visible its shape and style. The good news of the sermon is an essential component of this section. This is also the place where the preacher leads out the text biblically, exegetically, and contextually and applies it to the hearers.

3. *Conclusion:* This must be concise, and it should provide the opportunity for the hearers to capture the essence of both the good news and the message of the sermon so that these can take root in the hearts of the hearers.

The exercise of framing the outline can be a valuable tool for the preacher. Especially when one is caught up in the day-to-day activities of parish life, a brief moment taken to frame a possible outline of the sermon can go a long way to advancing the process of sermon development. In developing the outline, give as much attention to the contents and structure of the introduction and the conclusion as you do to the body of the sermon.

A good introduction prepares the hearers to receive the message of the sermon. For example, an introduction that makes reference to a familiar event, celebration, or concern may capture their immediate attention. Similarly, ending with a message of good news that is specific to the present lives of the congregation invites the hearers to go forward and do what they heard in the concluding moments of the sermon. A good conclusion encourages the hearers to go forward with the assurance that they can take the action and live out the message of the sermon through the grace of God that was offered in the good news of the sermon.

Whether it is expository or topical, the body of the sermon may be developed in any of several structures or styles.[1] The style of the sermon may be dictated by the scripture text on which it is based, but most often the preacher selects the style that will allow the text to be heard clearly and the message of the sermon to come alive to the hearers. Regardless of the style, the preacher selects the point at which the good news is presented in the sermon. In a deductive sermon, the preacher begins by naming the good news, which is then brought to life in the substance of the sermon. The sermon may also move inductively and present the good news at or close to the end of the sermon. By waiting until the end, the preacher invites the congregation to join the preacher on the journey that is the sermon and together with the preacher arrive at the anticipated outcome of hearing good news. Of the many recognized styles of sermons the most commonly used sermon styles are:

1. *The traditional sermon*—expository or topical—which moves sequentially using either (a) tasks or (b) points to arrive at its message.

2. *Puritan Plain Style*[2] is a biblical expository sermon that takes a text, performs an exposition and a theological analysis, and applies the interpretation of the text to the life of the congregation.

3. *The narrative* is a story that works through a plot to arrive at a particular resolution.

4. *The journey to celebration*, recognized as traditionally African American, is inherently dialogical and calls forth an emotive response to the biblical text in order to impact core beliefs.

5. *The Four Pages of the Sermon*[3] is a newer style that is aimed at encouraging more intentional biblical preaching.

In addition, there are specific styles that are directed by the contents of the biblical texts, such as parables that lean toward a narrative or story style or Psalms that favor a verse-by-verse style. I include the scripture text for ease of reference, as well as the good news and message statements developed from the text.

- *Scripture Text:* Mark 10:46–52

  [46] They came to Jericho. As he and his disciples and a large crowd were leaving Jericho, Bartimaeus son of Timaeus, a blind beggar, was sitting by the roadside. [47] When he heard that it was Jesus of Nazareth, he began to shout out and say, "Jesus, Son of David, have mercy on me!" [48] Many sternly ordered him to be quiet, but he cried out even more loudly, "Son of David, have mercy on me!" [49] Jesus stood still and said, "Call him here." And they called the blind man, saying to him, "Take heart; get up, he is calling you." [50] So throwing off his cloak, he sprang up and came to Jesus. [51] Then Jesus said to him, "What do you want me to do for you?" The blind man said to him, "My teacher, let me see again." [52] Jesus said to him, "Go; your faith has made you well." Immediately he regained his sight and followed him on the way.

- *Good News Statement:* Jesus Christ restores us to fullness of life.

- *Message Statement:* Don't give up on your hope for new life. Christ hears. Christ will restore your life.

SERMON STYLE 1A: TRADITIONAL SERMON THAT MOVES SEQUENTIALLY USING TASKS[4]

The keyword to this style of sermon is movement. The sermon must move in a step-by-step progression that leads recognizably to the culminating point where the hearers can receive the good news for themselves and accept the charge of the message of discipleship. A task refers to a particular action that the preacher must perform by using the words of the sermon to convince the hearers to adopt a particular position or belief and take action based on that belief. The substance of the belief is based on the good news of the sermon. For this sermon the goal of the preacher is to enable the hearers to believe and accept Christ's promise of a restored life for those who turn to Christ.

Task 1: Help the hearers to understand the reality of Bartimaeus' situation as a blind beggar in his society. The preacher must work to set aside the Western twenty-first-century image in order to understand more clearly what it meant to be blind in first-century Palestine. The need for restoration exists only when something has been lost. Bartimaeus' situation reported in the text as simply "sitting by the roadside" does not reflect the full meaning or picture of the devastating loss of place and even of self that being blind and a beggar represented at that time and place. Selective exegesis of the situation surrounding the blind man will allow hearers to understand the true condition of the man and the full meaning of his situation, which is essentially hopeless. The ultimate purpose of this task is to help persons who might be feeling hopeless to take stock of their situation in comparison to Bartimaeus'.

Task 2: Communicate the urgency of Bartimaeus' call for Jesus' attention and contrast the response of the people with Jesus' response. This may enable persons who see their lives as impossibly far removed from Jesus to be encouraged to reevaluate their position. In order to provide the full picture of the gap between Jesus and Bartimaeus instituted by society, frame the scene in which Jesus appears. Here also exegesis will provide important specifics that will improve understanding of the devastation to one's life in that community caused by blindness, and the depth of compassion demonstrated in Jesus' response to Bartimaeus' need. This task must make clearly apparent the true scope of Jesus' response and subsequent action with the purpose of encouraging those who feel separated from Christ to believe that nothing will prevent Jesus from responding to their need for restoration.

Task 3: Celebrate Bartimaeus' good news of the restoration of his sight and thereby his life in the community. The words of the text seem to make light of this momentous event; therefore, the preacher must work to bring alive the joy that Bartimaeus experienced at the restoration of his sight and therefore of his life in the society. His restoration is hope realized—hope that had little or no basis in reality, given the culture of the time and place, yet it was fulfilled. This is good news to be communicated with joy that causes the congregation to celebrate with Bartimaeus.

Task 4: Deliver the good news of Jesus' readiness to hear the cries of all those who represent Bartimaeus in their midst, and within the hearers themselves, and to offer restoration. This is the moment to which the sermon has been leading. It is the main point of the sermon—to offer the good news of divine grace. Make it as specific as possible and offer it with excitement and joy. This final task must bring home the message that Christ is listening for each person and stands ready to offer restoration for life, and that, therefore, like Bartimaeus, even with all signs to the contrary, one need not give up hope.

• • •

Using tasks to direct the work of sharing the good news and delivering the message requires the preacher to exegete the text carefully and pay particular attention to life situations that can connect with the hearers. Instead of reducing everything to a facile "tell Jesus and live" motto, use the sermon to offer authentic hope to some of life's situations through the mitigating, renewing love of Jesus Christ. In this way the sermon presents good news and calls the hearers to look at their own situations with renewed hope and faith.

SERMON STYLE 1B: TRADITIONAL SERMON THAT MOVES SEQUENTIALLY USING POINTS[5]

Despite the advances in homiletic form and the introduction of many new styles of sermons, many preachers (if not the majority) still preach most sermons in a style that makes points. To be effective, the points should also move the sermon sequentially to the good news. The general rule is three points that may contain subpoints, which in turn provide the substance of the sermon.

Point 1: Bartimaeus was a nonperson in the eyes of his society, as are many in the world, even among the hearers. This first point not only identifies Bartimaeus' location in time, but it brings into focus the re-identification or nonidentification each person may encounter depending on the location in which they find themselves. This first point connects the hearers with Bartimaeus by causing them essentially to sit with Bartimaeus out of the mainstream of life because of identity problems. There are many examples of current life situations that the preacher can use to make the point come alive.

Point 2: Jesus sees Bartimaeus and each person in the fullness of each one's personhood and reaches past all barriers to provide the life each person needs. The preacher can make the point of Jesus' concern for the least and the invisible among the crowds of life by using Jesus' call to Bartimaeus from the midst of the crowd. The point brings alive the good news that each person has value in the eyes of God, that Christ willingly and readily takes time to hear the cries of the forgotten and the silenced ones. This good news is specific and recognizable. Christ's recognition of the worth of every person at all the times and seasons of life is good news to be shared joyfully and earnestly.

Point 3: Because Jesus is ready to hear and answer every call, no one need give up hope even when it seems that life is passing us by. The preacher urges each hearer to remain hopeful in the face of life's difficulties through focusing faith in Christ. This is a reiteration of the good news but it is also a charge to the hearers to keep hope alive through the assurance of divine grace. This is the good news that permeates the message and is the main point of the sermon.

SERMON STYLE 2: PURITAN PLAIN STYLE

This style is simple and is aimed at helping the congregation to have the greatest possible encounter with the gospel. The exposition of the text is exegetical and the theological analysis deals specifically with the divine/human relationship as seen in the text. The application brings home the biblical text to the present community in quite specific terms. It is the moment in the sermon when the congregation says, "That preacher knows what it is like to be me," and may lead people to take action; or it may lead the hearers to joy, gratitude, silence, or prayer. It is the place where the preacher applies the good news for that unique time and place.

Exposition of the text: Bartimaeus' situation is typical for his time and place. In first-century Palestine, the blind were counted with the non-persons of society, which means that they were prevented from participating in some of the rituals of temple worship even though there were temple laws that provided protections for them. Jesus is on the way to Jerusalem for the last time on the way to the cross, and this is the final healing event before he enters the city.

Theological analysis: Interpreters suggest that the healing of the blind man is symbolic of the eventual healing of the blindness of the disciples who do not "see" Jesus as the Messiah. Bartimaeus in his physical blindness recognizes Jesus as the Son of David (which means Messiah) and so will the disciples eventually. Further, Jesus' response to Bartimaeus' cry for mercy and healing is also symbolic of Jesus' response to the cries of humanity for healing and restoration from sin. Bartimaeus' healing restores him to a place in the community.

Application: Jesus' response to Bartimaeus' nonperson situation and specifically the attention given to the man at a time when he is on the way to the cross offers hope for those who feel that life has pushed them to the sidelines and that no one, not even God, has time for them or will listen to their cries for mercy. The story gives them hope and even assurance that Jesus will hear their cries regardless of society's action to the contrary and that through Christ they will be restored to a full place in life and to wholeness of life.

By using specific examples of situations that are familiar to the community, the preacher makes the sermon real to the hearers and they connect with the good news of Christ's healing for their own lives and are able to go forward in the spirit of restoration and new life.

SERMON STYLE 3: NARRATIVE

In shaping the narrative sermon, Eugene Lowry's comparison to a novel offers a framework for the step-by-step process. He says the plot "begins with a felt *discrepancy* or conflict, and then makes its way through *complication* (things always get worse), makes a decisively sharp turn or *reversal*, and then moves finally toward *resolution*, or closure."[6] Certainly this story of Bartimaeus has all these elements and may be presented as a narrative sermon. The challenge for the preacher is not so much in the telling of the story, but in allowing the story to tell the good news of God's presence in the worst that life offers and God's readiness to restore or renew life for and in each person. The way that I frame this sermon outline follows Lowry's movements.

Discrepancy: Bartimaeus is a nonperson, invisible to and set aside because of his situation of being blind. Many in the world are relegated to nonperson status and become invisible because of their life situations. We can become nonpersons when we are out of our element or outside our comfort zone, and the feeling is devastating even if it is only for a time. Bartimaeus had no hope of being other than what society had named him, or of having what had been withheld from him, and yet he did not give up hoping.

Complication: Bartimaeus heard about Jesus' passing in his vicinity but had no chance of getting close or being heard because of the crowds. But he held on to hope and shouted for his life. His chance of being seen or heard was complicated by the presence of the crowd and by their demand that he stop shouting out to Jesus. Who or what causes us to stop trying to reach out to Jesus for healing and restoration? Sometimes the crowds are in our own hearts as we doubt that Jesus wants to hear us. This is a common complaint even among Christians, and it may be a place that connects the congregation with Bartimaeus' story.

Reversal: Jesus stops and calls for Bartimaeus. Even in the noise of the crowd, Jesus hears Bartimaeus and does not ignore him; he calls for him. Jesus listens for that lone voice and hears even a faint cry amid all the noises that work to drown it out. This is good news, especially for those who have kept silent for fear of not being heard, or of being heard and ignored or rejected. It speaks to the condition of many within and outside the church.

Resolution: Jesus restores Bartimaeus' sight. Hope is realized and there is great celebration. The message of good news comes alive in the celebration that follows the happy resolution of Bartimaeus' dream of new life. It is a testimony that speaks into the heart of those who still remain quiet, afraid to hope, afraid to call to Jesus, afraid to reach out for fear of rejection. Restoration of life is possible through Christ. Don't give up the hope and don't be afraid to call out; restoration in Christ is still available. The good news of Bartimaeus' restoration engenders hope for personal and communal restoration through Christ. And that is good news.

SERMON STYLE 4: JOURNEY TO CELEBRATION

The idea of a journey that moves to a celebrative conclusion fits as well to frame this story of Bartimaeus' restoration. Frank Thomas describes this process as "Celebration as Ecstatic Reinforcement."[7] This process moves the sermon through three stages, each with a specific emotional process and homiletic intent. The first is situation/complication, which stresses emotive logic with the homiletic goal of getting the people involved and identifying with the story. Cognitive logic is the emotional process that engages the second step of the process, which Thomas names as gospel assurance to complication, in which the good news of scripture serves the purpose of resolving the complication. Once this is done, the homiletic intent is that "emotive logic mandates that the preacher culminates the sermon by ecstatically reinforcing the good news through celebration."[8]

Bartimaeus is on a journey and it is emotion-packed as he strives to rise from his situation, to be heard by the one he believes is the only possible source for his restoration, and to triumph over all odds and regain a place in his society. It resonates with the situation of African Americans who are too often relegated to nonperson status, who are invisible to many, and who are commanded much too often to sit down and shut up. It fits also the intent of the celebrative model in calling the people to a model of Christian living that reaches out to Christ against all odds. The outline for this sermon may be framed as a series of steps, literal steps in the case of Bartimaeus, and figurative and spiritual steps in the case of the congregation. The goal is restoration of life in Jesus Christ. The preacher's focus is helping to direct the people on the journey that leads to the goal of fullness of life, restored through Jesus Christ. At each step the preacher performs a series of tasks that call the people to participate with Bartimaeus on his journey to restoration. Bartimaeus' journey is their journey, and the sermon helps the hearers to feel as Bartimaeus feels so that at the end they can rejoice as Bartimaeus rejoices. Using the stages as defined by Thomas, the journey of the sermon in three steps, each with a series of tasks, is as follows:

Step 1 (Situation/complication): This describes Bartimaeus' situation in detailed terms using the exegetical material that brings out the depth of meaning of his position as a blind beggar in that society. The preacher brings the people into the story to sit with Bartimaeus, or even to take on the identity of Bartimaeus. Thomas' emotive logic enables the situations of the text to be applied to the experiences of the people.

- Task A—Bring Bartimaeus' story alive by fleshing out his identity and situation.

- Task B—Set the scene of his placement in readiness for his encounter with Jesus.

- Task C—Connect Bartimaeus with the people by rephrasing his situation in the language of their situation: for example, Bartimaeus sitting by the roadside becomes a single mother sitting in the welfare office with her three small children running around her feet as she feeds a baby. She is a nonperson in the eyes of the people who would be troubled by her presence if they recognized her, so she is ignored.

Step 2 (Gospel assurance to complication): Bartimaeus' intent to reach Jesus and be healed is complicated because Jesus is surrounded by the disciples and the crowd, creating a physical distance that is comparable to the cultural distance put in place by the society. The crowd exacerbates the problem by trying to hush Bartimaeus' cries. Move the action along by bringing Jesus, the disciples, and the crowd into the picture.

- Task A—Set the scene by describing the following that Jesus has as he travels. Perhaps compare Jesus to present-day celebrities and the crowds of paparazzi that follow them. Allow Bartimaeus' voice to speak, first without being heard, then with the response of the crowd as being silent.

- Task B—Present Jesus' response to Bartimaeus as the aberration it was, given the norms of the society, and the divine grace it represents. Convert Bartimaeus' voice to the congregation's voice —individually and corporately. Use specific examples that will connect with the actual lives of the people.

- Task C—Apply Jesus' response to Bartimaeus to the lives of the people such that it becomes Jesus' response to each person and to the community. Put Jesus in the community walking through with his entourage and stopping to deal with the addict on the corner, the AIDS patient, the abused mother, the old man on the stoop.

Step 3 (Resolution/celebration): The resolution of Bartimaeus' situation comes with the good news (gospel) that Jesus hears him, calls to him, and heals him. This is good news worthy of celebration that reaches into the soul of every person who has been ignored or bypassed, whatever the cause. Celebrate Bartimaeus' restoration by naming the promise of restoration to every individual and to the whole community.

- Task A—Remind them that they—each one and the whole community—sit in Bartimaeus' seat, and that they can seek restoration for themselves and for the community by reaching out to Christ in the assurance that Jesus will hear and is ready to respond with affirmation that speaks of restoration.

- Task B—Celebrate Bartimaeus' restoration as that which is promised to each one who calls out to Jesus Christ. Celebrate the assurance that Christ answers the call of each person, hearing the voice, calling forth the person, restoring each in love. As appropriate, call out names of some of those present so that persons become invested in taking the journey to new life. Call and response is a common and familiar style of preaching in the African American worship tradition.

- Task C—Repeat the offer of new life and call the community forward to accept the gift. End with the good news that Christ stands waiting in their midst to restore each one to wholeness. The normal ending in African American churches is an altar call, and this may be done using phrasing from the sermon.

The blatant use of emotion is an important aspect of this model of preaching. Its presence is the expectation of most African American congregations and, when supported by good exegesis and an orderly approach to the goal of a triumphant Christ in the lives of the people, it elicits a deep spiritual response to the good news and to the message of the sermon.

SERMON STYLE 4: FOUR PAGES OF THE SERMON

Paul Scott Wilson's four-page model is both biblical and theological. The biblical facts of trouble and grace in the text are given a theological response that parallels the action of human sin and divine grace in the world. It speaks directly to the good news of God's grace, which triumphs over the trouble caused by human sin. Although pages 1, 2, and 3 may appear in any order, the necessity of presenting page 4 last becomes even more critical for the good news sermon. This model lends itself especially to good news preaching because of the juxtaposition of human sin and divine grace in the sermon.

The action of Bartimaeus' story is almost classic in its presentation of trouble and grace, and the preacher has the somewhat simple task of connecting the situation of the community with the situation of the Bible and the more difficult task of helping the congregation to experience Christ's active presence in their time of need, without making it a sinecure for whatever ails you. The motif of restoration as a consequence of action is an important element in the story that must be brought forward without allowing it to overshadow the free offering of divine grace. The description of the four pages follows, but the subsequent outline used to create a complete sermon will show how they have been used to offer good news in the sermon.

Page 1—Trouble in the Bible: Bartimaeus is on the Jericho Road—a dangerous place. Bartimaeus is blind and a beggar (the two often went hand in hand)—a dangerous life. In fact, Bartimaeus has no real life since he lives outside the community. He is a nonperson who must be silenced when he attempts to speak out and get Jesus' attention.

Page 2—Trouble in the World: Name the many persons in the world whom Bartimaeus represents. Give examples from the community and the larger world society. Provide examples that capture individuals and groups who have become nonpersons in the eyes of their community or the world. Name their need for restoration to fullness of life.

Page 3—God's Grace in the Bible: Jesus hears Bartimaeus, stops, and calls for him. Jesus connects with him by speaking directly to him and asking about his need. Jesus heals him and restores him to community.

Jesus' action is not simply about healing; by speaking directly to Bartimaeus he also recognizes and honors his identity. Jesus' action is in response to Bartimaeus' need.

Page 4—God's Grace in the World: Jesus hears and has heard the calls from each person. Jesus speaks—is ready to speak—directly to each one. Jesus responds—is ready to respond—to each person's need. Jesus offers restoration of life to each person—the good news. The substance of restoration is in response to the need and it is individual. Jesus restores each one to fullness of life.

THE FOUR-PAGE SERMON: AN EXAMPLE

SCRIPTURE TEXT: Mark 10:46–52

GOOD NEWS STATEMENT: Jesus Christ restores us to fullness of life.

MESSAGE STATEMENT: Don't give up on your hope for new life. Christ will restore your life.

SERMON TITLE: The Road to Restoration

CONTEXT OF PREACHING: Tuesday chapel service at the Chapel of the Unnamed Faithful at Garrett-Evangelical Theological Seminary. Tuesday chapel services are formal services of Word and Table that use the lectionary readings for the coming Sunday.

OUTLINE:

> *Introduction:* The movie *Dreamer*—a story of restoration of an entire community—summarization of the background of the story and transition to the text by using the idea of the Jericho Road as a road leading to restoration.

Page 1: Trouble in the Bible

- Bartimaeus on the Jericho Road is a nonperson in the eyes of his society.
  - the Jericho Road—poverty and danger—the road to Jerusalem where danger and restoration (to his vicinity) awaits Jesus
  - Bartimaeus' situation—blind, a beggar = a nonperson in the eyes of the community

Page 2: Trouble in the World

- Nonpersons continue to exist in society today. Give examples of present-day situations that relegate individuals or groups to nonperson status.
  - Old married couple with no one to care for their needs
  - Down's syndrome grocery bagger
  - Victimized groups around the world
  - Each person in an unfamiliar situation

Page 3: God's Action in the Bible

- Jesus hears and responds to Bartimaeus' need with divine grace.
  - Bartimaeus calls out in hope; Jesus hears, stops
  - Jesus acknowledges Bartimaeus' personhood; calls him; speaks directly to him; allows him to state his need
  - Jesus heals Bartimaeus and restores him to community
  - Restored Bartimaeus rejoices, follows Jesus

Page 4: God's Action in the World

- Jesus invites us to tell him our needs and is ready to restore us to wholeness.
  - Recognize the challenge of calling out our need
  - Call in hope and faith that Jesus is listening, will hear and respond
  - Baptism has put us on the road to restoration = good news
  - The joy of our restoration will allow us to follow Christ to eternity

Conclusion:

- Tie in the end of the movie *Dreamer* and the restoration of the community plus an invitation to the good news of personal restoration through Christ.
  - Restate the promise of Christ to respond to our needs
  - Give assurance of Jesus' presence, listening, offering restoration
  - End with good news of restoration of life for eternity through Jesus Christ

THE SERMON:

Introduction:

> You are a great champion.
> When you ran the ground shook;
> The sky opened and mere mortals parted.
> Parted the way to victory
> Where you'll meet me in the winner's circle
> And I'll put a blanket of flowers on your back.

In the movie *Dreamer*, Cale Crane speaks these words into her horse's ear and heart before the filly, Sonador (or Dreamer), runs in Kentucky's prestigious Breeders' Cup race. The hopes and dreams of this little girl and of her entire community are anchored in this horse and this race. Cale's immediate community is comprised of her retired horseman grandfather, once a successful breeder of thoroughbred horses; her father, almost broken in spirit and out of work; her mother, who has watched her dreams die; the jockey, who lives with the fear of falling and being seriously hurt in another race; and the trainer, who has no other job and nothing else to train but this single horse. This horse that they are all depending on, and in whom Cale has such deep faith, has already broken a bone in its leg and was almost put down a few months earlier.

Last week as I lived into the process of sermon preparation that I teach my students, this movie *Dreamer* was the strongest of the whispers that infiltrated my mind and my spirit. Two themes in particular in the movie captured my attention. The first was the obvious need for restoration of the community and the second was the almost tangible evidence of a lived faith. And I came to realize that the all-important race that Sonador would run was in reality the community's "Road to Restoration."

Page 1: Trouble in the Bible

The passage of scripture that we heard read from Mark 10 puts us on a different road. It is the Jericho Road, a much traveled, even dangerous, route to Jerusalem, as Jesus implied in his Good Samaritan parable. The biblical record informs us that Jesus came from Galilee to Jerusalem by way of the Jordan Valley and the city of Jericho. Jesus' familiarity with this road is evidenced by his several activities in and around Jericho, which scholars believe were most likely associated with the poorer section of the city—no surprise there. So in this text it is also no surprise to find Jesus on the way to Jerusalem by way of the Jericho Road.

Poor and blind, begging for his living, Bartimaeus is also on the road, or rather at the side of the road. Most likely he has a particular spot where he is taken to each day in the hope that he will catch the attention of some traveler with enough substance to give him a coin or two. He has no place in society except as a roadside beggar. Although there are covenantal protections afforded him that prevent others from deliberately misleading him or causing him to stumble, because of his blindness he is also prevented from making the sacrifices to God that were intrinsic to his culture and religion.

His name tells us that he has a connection with a parent, a father —Bar-timaeus, son of Timaeus—but the normal trappings of family life—wife and children—are lost to him and he is such a nonperson that in Matthew 20:29–34 and Luke 18:35–43, the parallel versions of this story, he is unnamed. His blindness is a blemish, a disqualifier (as *Harper's Bible Dictionary* defines it) from active participation in certain societal and temple activities. Although we do not know whether or not his condition began at his birth, now he has been relegated to the sidelines, out of sight. In the eyes of the community around him, he is considered at best a nuisance, but most people simply do not see him.

So having become alert to Jesus' presence in his vicinity, Bartimaeus begins to cry out for Jesus' attention. It is no surprise that the crowd tries to shut him up. The blind should keep out of the way and beggars should neither be seen nor heard. Certainly a blind beggar, recognizably a sinner under divine punishment, should not draw attention to himself and he should not be allowed to bother important people like the Rabbi. If anything, blind beggars need to move out of the way so that real people, people who matter, people of value, can pass undisturbed. Be quiet, Bartimaeus; nobody wants to see you.

Page 2: Trouble in the World

There are so many Bartimaeuses around us, so many that we prefer not to see because of their nuisance value. The old couple, married for sixty years, has buried their only child and now lives in the house on the corner with the overgrown yard, broken stoop, and unpainted, peeling shutters. They come out together to the grocery store, moving slowly, shuffling along. He cannot leave her alone because a combination of dementia and some stage of Alzheimer's causes her to open doors and walk away. So she holds on to him as he makes his way up the aisle, and everyone within a six-foot radius holds his or her nose. She has soiled herself. No one wants to look at them. They have lost their identity as full persons and in the minds of most have been relegated to the side of the road, preferably out of sight.

Or there's the Down's syndrome man, old yet still a child, who attempts to bag the groceries but senses disapproval—or is it fear?—from the customer. So he becomes even more clumsy than usual and begins to talk loudly to himself as he tries to gather his scattered wits. And those around him steal a glance at him and look away, seeing only incompetence and inability, not the child of God for whom they pray unthinkingly in church. He too they relegate to the status of nonperson for whom there is no worthwhile place in the community.

And then there are whole groups who become faceless and nameless, nonpersons, because it's too difficult to deal with them. It's easy to feel overwhelmed when we hear of the genocide in Rwanda, Kosovo, and Darfur, of the millions that have been killed in ethnic purging. It's beyond overwhelming to hear of the pandemic of AIDS in Africa and even in some communities in America. The commercials that feature poor, starving children around the world tug at our heartstrings; sometimes it is easier to turn off the TV than to acknowledge the individual persons who have lost their places and their value in the community of the world. It's more than most of us can cope with, so we try to avoid seeing them or dealing with them, in part by denying their personhood.

But somehow we fail to see ourselves in that same light. I think most if not all of us here would not consider ourselves as nonpersons, as persons of less than full value or of no value. And yet, there's a Bartimaeus in each of us. Said another way, each of us may be Bartimaeus in some context. Somewhere, someone looks at us and devalues us, tells us verbally or even by a look to shut up, that we don't have sufficient value to be heard, whether because of our age, gender, ability, sexual orientation, or some other value-laden identifier. Or it may be something as simple as location: a store clerk, or an airline attendant, or a bank employee, because of our lack of situational knowledge, acts as though we are totally brainless or stupid. Simply because we are not in a place of relevant knowledge, someone tries to tell us that we are a nuisance and should be quiet. We are out of our familiar place and therefore unworthy of being heard. In those moments we become nonpersons in their eyes; we become Bartimaeus, a blind beggar, calling out, wanting to be recognized as the full persons we are.

Page 3: God's Action in the Bible

Bartimaeus called out to Jesus. In the face of a hostile crowd trying to silence him, Bartimaeus persisted. He kept calling and Jesus heard. Jesus, who came to bring good news to the poor, to offer release to all in captivity, recovery of sight to the blind, and freedom to the oppressed, heard and saw Bartimaeus. Jesus, whose mission was that of restoration, stopped. He was busy about the business of salvation for the whole world; he was on his way to Jerusalem to give his life as a ransom for all people; yet in the midst of a schedule much busier than any we could undertake, he stood still and called for Bartimaeus.

Can you imagine the joy that flooded Bartimaeus' soul when he was urged to get up because Jesus was calling him? I can see him springing up, throwing off the cloak that he had used to protect himself from the elements and even to hide himself from being noticed by the wrong people. There he is, hands outstretched, reaching out to Jesus, reaching out to the community, reaching out for restoration, for life, reaching out in hope and faith that the healer he had heard so much about in the conversations of the travelers on that Jericho Road would grant him his desire. You see, that day when Bartimaeus took his place on the Jericho Road, he had no idea that the well-known roadway would become his road to restoration. But Jesus heard Bartimaeus, and Jesus called for him.

Bartimaeus came armed with his faith. He came with the expectation that Jesus would recognize and respond to his need. He came believing that his faith would be rewarded. And Jesus, even though he knew what Bartimaeus needed, even with his divine sight that perceived better than Bartimaeus what his restoration required, asked the blind beggar to name his need. There was no presumption on the part of our Savior. Instead he asked, "What do you want me to do for you?" Bartimaeus understood his blindness and knew what he most required for his life in the future. "My teacher, let me see again."

It was a request that came from the depth of his being, and Jesus responded with an affirmation—not simply an affirmation of Bartimaeus' request, but of his faith. Jesus heard and understood Bartimaeus' words as a cry for more than physical sight. The restoration of his sight would restore him to full personhood, to community, to life in all its fullness. "Go; your faith has made you well." Jesus heard Bartimaeus' need at its deepest level and granted his request. Jesus provided restoration to this blind beggar who, having regained his sight, having experienced his own restoration, joined Jesus on our Savior's road to the restoration of all humanity. Unlike many who had walked with Jesus, even the disciples, Bartimaeus' spiritual sight enabled him to see the Christ; and, with his physical sight restored, he could join the crowd and follow Jesus on the way to the cross.

Page 4: God's Action in the World

My sense is that some of us are not yet in the place where we can name our need for restoration. Some of us do not believe that we can be identified with Bartimaeus. But isn't that why Jesus came? Did we not lose our identity as full persons of God because of sin? That's the legacy of our birth, and when we all come to that recognition and understand our need for restoration we too can cry out to Jesus. Jesus is already listening to hear our cries and Jesus is waiting to restore each of us to fullness of life with God.

There's a whole lot that exists in the world, in our society, even in the church that may work to prevent us from seeking the restoration that Christ offers. But if we can acknowledge our sinfulness, receive the forgiveness and claim the new birth that Christ offers, then we're on the road. Our baptism in Christ is the starting point that gives us new sight and names us, like the restored Bartimaeus, as followers of Jesus Christ. And through the grace of God, by faith in the promise of Christ to be with us every step of the way, we can stay on the road that leads to total restoration with God. God gives us grace freely to keep our faith alive and strong, so that, like Bartimaeus, we can cry out to Jesus in the assurance that Jesus will hear and answer our cries.

Bartimaeus' joy when he heard that Jesus was calling him is nothing compared to the joy that we can experience when we come boldly to Christ, knowing that he can and will restore us to our place with God for all eternity. Jesus offers restorative grace that makes us whole. And when we allow that restoration to take place within us, then and only then can we follow Christ faithfully on the journey that leads to life eternal. Then and only then can we work to ensure that the full personhood of each and every person is valued. Then and only then can each of us, and all of us, follow in his footsteps and be about our Savior's business of restoration for the whole world.

Conclusion

Despite all kinds of setbacks, Sonador, a horse once given up for dead, ran the prestigious race. It was a comeback the likes of which the racing world had never seen. The faith of her child owner was rewarded. Sonador won the Breeders' Cup and they placed a blanket of flowers on her back. Grandfather, father, mother, jockey, and trainer all had their hopes met, and they rejoiced. And, yes, it is a movie, a feel-good movie, the kind I like best, so, yes, the happy ending is what I expected. But ending with Jesus Christ takes us beyond anything the movies have to offer.

Jesus Christ fulfills all our hopes beyond our expectations. Jesus Christ restores our life now and for eternity. All we need, individually and collectively, is the faith that his grace affords us, and by his word we can be restored. Perhaps someone here is sitting at the side of her or his own Jericho Road, staring blindly into nothingness, perhaps even glad to be overlooked, or maybe hoping that something will change in her or his life for the better. Well, if you are that someone, Jesus is walking by. Call out to him; call out in faith. Perhaps you have been trying to reach Jesus, but many things are getting in the way; keep calling, Jesus is listening. Be persistent, Jesus will hear you. Jesus will restore your life for all eternity.

Thanks be to God.

six

■

Delivering the Sermon as a
Good News Message

lthough I have several books of sermons, have studied large numbers of written sermons, and even wrote my dissertation on the sermons of John Wesley, I find it difficult to get enthusiastic about reading sermons. Generally my mind wanders trying to imagine how the preacher told the story, or expressed the urgency of the material, or encouraged participation of the congregation in the proclamation of the word. Preaching is a spoken art, and the road between text and proclamation, between developing and preaching the sermon, is long and tricky and littered with many ideas, practices, and methods of presentation that did not work.

In my classes I stress the importance of pulpit presence, and students are evaluated on presentation and delivery of their sermons almost as much as they are on the structure and content of each sermon. The ideas in this book are ones that I have used in my seminary classes, but without being actually present with you to demonstrate what I am hoping to teach, it becomes difficult to put them into words and troublesome to imagine that someone might be misled or misdirected as that person reads into or out of the ideas in this chapter erroneous or contrary advice.

This chapter addresses several areas of the preaching task that affect both the delivery and the receipt of the sermonic message.

Language, like preaching, is always contextual, and the preacher's language combined with the language of the sermon (they are not necessarily the same) must resonate with the language of the hearers if they are to hear a message of good news from the mouth of the preacher. In addition, the preacher's imagination, a gift of God, in tandem with the work of the Holy Spirit, helps to make sermons listenable. On many occasions I have heard sermons that have been delivered in a tone and pitch that have convinced many that they represent the work of the Holy Spirit but that not only contained no good news, but were also weak in content and shaky in structure. On the other hand, I have heard many sermons that have been erudite and well structured but that have been delivered in such a joyless, unenthusiastic manner that the congregation—those who were not asleep—simply ignored the preacher as they gazed out with unfocused eyes. Obviously we need balance; and as a contextual art, preaching that is effective in one culture or congregation is not necessarily effective in another. The impact of the setting on the efficacy of the sermon is an essential ingredient and is something I will also address.

Preaching is a liturgical act that takes place in the midst of the gathered community. As preachers, we consider the location of preaching in order to accommodate the fit between the sermon, the style of presentation, and the response of the hearers. I love alliteration, and it occurred to me that in addressing the subject of sermon delivery I could reduce it to three major areas: language, location, and looks. The ultimate purpose of this chapter is to impress upon preachers the importance of good delivery in good news preaching. Good news preaching requires both development and delivery that take seriously the understanding of preaching as the act of proclaiming the gospel of divine grace.

LANGUAGE

In the foreword to Ronald Sleeth's text *God's Word and Our Words*, Thomas Long writes, "because God's Word finds expression in human speech, it can never be confined to the cultus, but moves to embrace the world. It can never be frozen and codified into a set of principles or eternal verities but remains alive, active, dynamic."[1] In short, words matter. Words are a dynamic expression of the culture, ever changing, ever being created, ever reframed in their use. Keeping abreast of the descriptive words that speak to a culture is essential to preachers because words change with the passing of each day.

In the movie *Akeelah and the Bee,* a story about words, Akeelah is challenged by her coach about the use of a slang word. Her response is to open the latest version of the dictionary and respond with the recorded definition of said word. She reminds her teacher (and every preacher who understands and appreciates the value of words in the sermon, that language is a living art. To put a slightly different slant on Ronald Sleeth's words, "it should be good news that the words [original Word] they preach [are] alive and dynamic and . . . can be a means of grace."[2] I make the change unapologetically because we preach the Word only as the Holy Spirit transforms the words that we speak.

The language of the sermon must not only be contextually dynamic, it must be easily understood. The congregation, even when it consists of biblical scholars, does not have the time, and certainly not the inclination, to translate the language of the sermon into ordinary language. The sermon is not an academic paper and, although we worship God with heart *and* mind, the sermon is (or must be) aimed at the heart if it is going to affect the hearers spiritually for their Christian discipleship. The caveat to this directive is the problem of talking down to the community. While the hearers of the sermon may be the children of God, they are not all children in age, and they deserve the respect of the preacher who, though seminary trained and even scholarly, is on equal footing in the eyes of God, whose Word we are all called to preach. The language of the seminary is not the language of the church in its identity as the gathered community. The words of the classroom or the scholar do not represent the language of the people in the pews. And while seminary teaches us important theological words "and our listeners are certainly able to learn what they mean, it can be frustrating when a preacher sprinkles the sermon with 'theologese,' either forgetting that others do not speak that language or trying to impress the listeners with how learned he or she is."[3]

CONVERSATIONAL LANGUAGE

Preaching is not merely dialogical (that is, between two persons), it is (or should be) conversational. The preacher engages in a three-way conversation with God and the people of God. And, in fact, since there is truly no single corporate voice in the church, the conversation partners have the ability to multiply exponentially as more hearers/speakers enter the realm of the conversation engaged by the preacher through the sermon. Lucy Rose offers a conversational mode of preaching in which, "by realizing that although *one* may do the speaking, the preacher is never isolated or alone."[4] The conversational sermon invites the hearers to reflect and respond not simply to the preacher but to the words as well. Wes Allen, following Rose's lead, notes that in conversational preaching, "preachers, out of the depths of their convictions and experiences, propose a tentative interpretation of scripture and of the life of the congregation for the additions, corrections, and counter proposals."[5] This sounds suspiciously like the talk-back format of the African American church! Where the African American church's talk to the preacher is in support of that very kerygmatic expression named by Rose, a conversational approach invites substantive dialogue with the preacher of the Word of God.

What does this do for the good news aspect of the sermon? If the preacher is the one speaking on behalf of the many, and especially on behalf of God, then the preacher's conversation, the sermon, must be representative of the covenantal connection that is divine grace, which is the requirement and center of every sermon. Good news preaching cannot thus be other than conversational since the divine/human relationship that the preacher expounds is not limited to the preacher. The whispers of God that nudge us to proclaim the good news of divine grace are not directed only to the ears, heart, or mind of the preacher. God's Word comes to every person, "meets our condition, emerging quietly and most often unnoticeably in the midst of who and where we are."[6] And when it comes, perceived or not, it requires engagement by the preacher to become the proclaimed Word that invites celebration of the good news of God's redeeming grace for all people.

INCLUSIVE LANGUAGE

Although the use of inclusive language in writing and in public speaking is required at my seminary, the majority of students who enter my second year class preach with a mouthful of exclusive words. Both women and men of the church still find it difficult to speak inclusively about the divine. Some mistakenly (in my opinion) change to a feminine pronoun for God in the hope that it will be taken as a sign of their inclusivity of speech. And while I understand the intent and appreciate how unwieldy the words of the sermon can become when one tries to avoid the use of pronouns—whether masculine or feminine—when referring to God, there is seldom a time when I do not call the student to account for the misuse of language.

The good news of divine grace is that it is open and available to all. It is God's precious gift to the people of God—not gender selective, and not color blind. God in divine wisdom made us male and female, in all colors of the earth, for God's glory. In God's mind there is no barrier of language or origin that separates us from God. The good news is for all equally, and each individually. Those who still balk at the requirement and who use noninclusive language for God or for human beings are, wittingly or not, supporting separation or discrimination that is not good news. Exclusive language for God and people makes of the church a hierarchical, unjust entity. Unfortunately, that way of identifying God remains in use in many places and by many people, some happily and unapologetically. But, despite claims to the contrary, there cannot be good news in such places. The source of divine grace is also the seat of justice, and exclusivity among the people of God speaks of injustice that is contrary to the love of God.

The language of the church, the language of the preacher, and the language of good news preaching can so easily be representative of the love of God, and therefore inclusive. The preacher is commissioned to lead the church, and to engage the hearers in the open conversation initiated or continued by the sermon. If God is a welcome part of that conversation—and God must be if it is to have substance for the life of the people of God—then the name of God and the name of all the people of God must be said without equivocation or the segregation that noninclusive language supports and promotes. Preaching is an act of the church, and good news preaching is located only in the church that acknowledges and lives into the reality of unfettered grace. Paul asked, "What are we to say? Should we continue in sin in order that grace may abound? By no means!" (Rom. 5:1). Can the church or the preacher continue to exclude the people of God because of language? By no means. Good news preaching requires language that is graceful and meets the context of the place and people who represent the inclusive body of Christ.

LOCATION

Preaching is an act of the church. For the most part, preaching occurs in the context of church worship services and is a prominent part of the service. "What might our sermons be if preachers seriously acknowledged the Church?"[7] This important question framed by Richard Lischer calls preachers to understand more clearly their responsibility to the life of the church—that is, to more clearly offer good news that can make a difference in individual lives and in the life of the gathered community.

We explored the contextualization of the sermon in chapter 2, within the subject of exegeting the congregation. Recognizing that God breaks into our history and the history of the church, and being fully aware of our past, present, and the ever (and more quickly) changing future, we believe "God who works incarnationally, weaves the past together in fresh and redemptive ways moment by moment."[8] That means that there is always good news and the church is the place of proclamation of the good news. This is why not only do our sermons address the reality of the congregation's situation, but why, at every event of preaching, we preachers are called to offer the grace of God new again to the people. When we do this we reveal once again who God is for us in the present. That is good news preaching!

PREACHING IN THE PLACE OF WORSHIP

Worship reveals God. Preaching proclaims the Word of God, and through that proclamation God is revealed. Thus preaching and worship stand together. Preaching occurs in the context and location of worship, and preaching is an act of worship. Charles Rice suggests that the connection between preaching and the gathered community may be strengthened liturgically in part because "more attention to liturgy might well change the way we preach."[9] Liturgy is the work of the people; it is worship of God offered in community. And the preaching of the church takes place in the community of the people of God gathered for worship. The preacher stands in the action of remembering that binds the community. Through the words of the sermon, the preacher invites the people to participate actively in remembering God's grace, receiving that grace for themselves, and participating in the work of grace in the world. Preaching that is located in the context of worship has corporate ownership and responsibility. It is the people's representation of the Word of God alive in the place where God reveals God's self.

Worship as God's self-revelation and the people's response calls forth an equal response from the preacher as from the people. This is why the worship centers of initiating and sustaining grace—the baptismal font and the communion table—are best located in full view of the place of proclamation—lest the preacher lose sight of his or her own need for the same grace that is offered in the sermon. As Rice notes, "the preacher stands in the same place where every Christian is placed and formed . . . and it is this same reality that forms the preacher and that tests each sermon."[10] Good news preaching offers a reminder to the gathered community—including the preacher—that every person stands in need of covenantal grace, and that each is a recipient of divine grace. The proclamation of the good news serves as a reminder to the whole people of God that grace abounds. It is good news preached to, by, and for the whole people of God. It is the liturgy of the church, located in the context of the worship life of the church.

PREACHING AS ECCLESIAL SYMBOL

Preaching is a symbol of the church. That means that preaching is connected first and foremost with the church, and the expectation of preachers is generally that they will engage the art of preaching within a church building or a worship service that is connected with the church. Like other symbols of the Christian faith, such as the sacraments, preaching is symbolic of the mission and ministry of the church of Jesus Christ. The church exists wherever and whenever the people of God gather to celebrate the presence of God in their individual and corporate lives. Preaching the Word of God occurs in the gathering of the people, and as such it is symbolic of the active, enduring presence of God.

As a symbol of the church, good news preaching reminds the people of God's creative, redemptive, and transformative presence. Good news preaching testifies to the enduring grace of God that is at the heart of the interaction of God and humanity. Good news preaching symbolizes the presence of God revealed through the words of the sermon, which, through preaching, become the Word of God.

LOOKS

By looks I do not mean one's features or size, although our society is such that even preachers are prejudged based on both of those characteristics. What I am referring to is how a preacher uses his or her body to impart the message of good news. Regardless of one's physical state, the preacher must work to prevent that physical state from distracting hearers from receiving the message. The preacher's presence is a critical ingredient in making the sermon truly a message of good news.

EMBODIMENT OF THE SERMON

The story is told of the preacher who wagered that in the same sermon he could cause half the congregation to weep copiously and the other half to laugh hysterically. He won the wager by attaching a tail to the back of his pants, and as he preached a stirring, highly emotive sermon to the congregation facing one side of the church, his tail bobbed up and down, causing raucous laughter from those on the other side. Suffice it to say that his was not a faithful embodiment of the sermon. Preaching and listening to sermons are both multisensory activities, and while the preacher's task is not wringing a particular emotion from the listening congregation, the congregation is affected by the way in which the preacher embodies the sermon. The delivery of the good news sermon is as important as its creation.

The preacher therefore does well to be attentive to the need to engage the hearer to see, hear, touch, taste, and even smell the grace of

God. The senses with which God gifted us are so important in experiencing God's gift of life that when one sense is lost, another tries to compensate for the lost sense. It is almost common knowledge that persons who have lost their sight have sharper hearing. The savvy preacher considers the different ways in which people receive information and the importance of preaching to all the senses of the hearers. Such preachers also pay attention to the issues of life that may overshadow or mute the words of the sermon.

The movement of the whole body gives substance to the embodiment of the message of good news. For example, the voice utters the words that become Word; the eyes, windows of the soul, reveal the preacher's inner conviction of God's love and the commitment to sharing with and inviting others into that love; the gestures give expression of both invitation and conviction; and the body's movement demonstrates the energy of God's sustaining power that gives strength to the work of proclamation. Our body language sends a message along with or in contradiction to the words we speak. The preacher who in offering good news in the sermon looks and acts in a way that demonstrates that he or she is also the recipient of the good news will present a more believable sermon to the hearers.

Divine grace is good news worth shouting from the housetops! The preacher who comes dragging into the pulpit and reads from a manuscript with little or no expression and even less energy cannot hope to deliver any kind of good news to the congregation, regardless of what is written in the sermon or how well the good news message is expressed. Since the demeanor of the preacher lacks credibility, the people cannot hear the words.

The embodiment of the sermon speaks in part to the preacher's knowledge of the words of the sermon, but it speaks even more clearly to the preacher's own faith in and acceptance of the message of grace that the sermon offers. During their practice preaching, many students become self-conscious about their bodies and are sometimes excessively concerned about their pulpit presence. Yet many of those same students resist the idea that preachers could or should practice their delivery, and they express unnecessary discomfort through the entire sermon. In some cases students are stricken by vocal mannerisms that are so distracting that these become the listeners' focus. As human beings we are connected in mind, body, and spirit, and all three elements of our being must be engaged in preaching. The good news of the sermon is a gift of divine grace, and we preach it best when we are the embodiment of the good news of God's grace for all people.

DISTRACTIONS FROM THE MESSAGE OF GOOD NEWS

Any distraction to the sermon, whether it is the way we use our voice, hands, eyes, or any other part of the physical body, means that the words of the sermon take second place in the act of preaching, and the message to the hearers is filtered through any and all distractions. Some hearers may still receive the good news and may still hear the call to discipleship, but undoubtedly some will be unable to focus because of the distractions, and still others may abandon the effort to try to discern good news. So the preacher does well to pay attention to sermon delivery and body language.

The preacher's attire also speaks a language that either supports or denies the grace of God resident in the life and work of the preacher. Let me say clearly that I am not advocating cassocks, robes, suits, dresses, clergy collars, or any particular style of dress; I am simply noting that one's attire becomes part of the language of one's office, an element of body language, if you will, and the inappropriately clad body can be an unnecessary distraction.

Many preachers (especially student preachers) struggle to know what to do with their hands. For some, good or appropriate gestures do not come naturally or easily. Some students have complained that practicing in a mirror does not work since they look stiff. Good presentation most often comes with good knowledge of the sermon and the conviction that its message is true. The preacher who knows the material is free to concentrate on sharing the message of the sermon with the congregation and finds there is little or no need to be concerned with his or her hands. In fact the hands take on a life of their own as they also participate in getting the message of good news across to the people. I consider this the work of the Holy Spirit.

Other distractions to the delivery of good news during preaching occur through extraneous mouth sounds (for example, uh, ah, um) and movements or mannerisms such as clearing the throat often, repeatedly touching the ears or nose, or pushing back hair or spectacles. When these distractions occur, the content and especially the good news of the sermon can be lost. Good news preaching calls the preacher to embody the sermon, to make eye contact with the people to whom the message is directed, to show belief and excitement about the good news.

One final area of distraction is that of the sermon manuscript or notes. I have no preference for either manuscript or notes and have seen preachers preach just as well from both as a few do without either. And although I have had someone write to me to ask for my help in teaching preachers how to preach without a manuscript, I do believe that most hearers are not overly concerned about the issue. A problem arises when the preacher fumbles with the manuscript or notes, loses his or her place, and generally makes a big show of turning over pages of material. I teach students to make a fold at the corner of each page that will facilitate their grasp of the page so they may easily slide it to the side. In this way there is little to distract either the people or the preacher.

In most African American churches, pulpit stewards or persons who prepare the worship space provide water for the preacher. Some preachers are plagued by dryness of the mouth and need a drink of water to aid in their delivery of the sermon. As bottled water has become more and more popular, some preachers have begun to place a bottle of water in the pulpit for their use. Unfortunately, the sight of a bottle lifted to the mouth and head tilted back to take a drink presents a very different and generally uncomplimentary and distracting picture than a glass lifted to one's lips.

As we become more visually oriented, more and more preachers use video clips or still pictures in their sermons. This can be a distraction when the video clip is out of sync with the words of the sermon. The people cannot connect the two and easily give up one for the other, thereby missing a part of the message. When the preacher makes the choice to control the video from the pulpit, said preacher too often becomes caught up in preaching and forgets to advance the supporting material. In addition, if video clips are left too long on screen, the flow of the sermon is interrupted and this causes a distraction for the hearers. What is of primary importance in preaching is that the preacher take all the steps necessary in both the development and the delivery of the sermon to ensure that the gospel comes alive to the people and that the good news of God's grace is seen and heard and ultimately lived by preacher and people—the whole people of God.

CONCLUSION

I believe that every preacher is responsible for offering the good news of divine grace every time he or she preaches. That grace is the only hope that anyone has of overcoming sin, and preachers who have accepted the task of proclaiming that good news do so by the very grace of God he or she preaches. As preachers we speak of divine justice and mercy, and through the words of the sermon we offer both a warning against sin and death, and an invitation to life, both present and future, through God's redeeming grace. Preparing a sermon often resembles a balancing act as the preacher strives to offer realistic and visible good news of God's transformative grace without bypassing the critical and similarly responsible act of alerting the hearers to the sin that is present and visible in human life. Good news preaching keeps in focus the saving, enlivening presence of God that justifies and sanctifies repentant humanity. While the sermon as a medium of presenting this good news and the preacher as the proclamatory voice are critical ingredients in sharing the good news with the people, it is the Holy Spirit who gives life to the content of good news for both preacher and hearers.

When we accept scripture as the inspired Word of God and give careful attention to biblical interpretation, we can connect the written contents of scripture with the content of the lives of the hearers. Many preachers successfully motivate their hearers to live better lives, but only scripture provides proof positive of God's concern for and engagement with the lives of ordinary people in a way that has stood the test of time. Applying scriptural truths to human life through God's grace is what motivates and sustains hearers throughout their lives.

The good news preacher willingly delves into all of scripture to unearth the enlivening, sustaining presence of God in the past, connects it with the present lives of the people, and presents it as future promise and hope. But the words become Word for both preacher and hearers only through the transforming presence of the Holy Spirit. In ongoing conversation with the people the preacher may discern the effectiveness of his or her preaching. Appendix E offers a simple form that may be used to receive immediate feedback on preached sermons.

Hearers can tell when the preacher understands their situation in part by the way in which the preacher presents God's grace in the sermon. Divine grace is good news for everyone, but the application of God's grace to the situation of preaching gives the assurance that God's presence in the midst of the people relates directly to their needs and their hopes. Even in the face of the world's sin and degradation, the good news preacher keeps hope alive by preaching the good news of grace.

As preachers we experience the presence of the Holy Spirit in prayer and through our witness to God's grace, and this gives credence to the words of our sermons. At the heart of the sermon is the grace of God. The good news of the sermon is not merely the interpretation of a scripture text or topic brought to life through in-depth study, or even particularly the preacher's internalization of the Word and connection with the hearers. And although we may preach the good news that we have experienced in our relationship with God, the good news of our sermons is not about us. It is about God's grace present and available to all people for all time. And when we offer it to the people of God in our sermons—that's good news preaching.

four
good news
sermons

IT'S ALL ABOUT LOVE

This sermon was preached at the Wednesday Evening Gospel Service at Garrett-Evangelical Theological Seminary.

SCRIPTURE TEXTS: Isaiah 35:1–10 (CEV); Luke 1:46–50

SERMON STYLE: Topical Sermon in a Celebrative Style

GOOD NEWS STATEMENT: God's love restores us for joyful praise.

In the movie *I am Sam* a mentally retarded man is left to raise his baby girl, Lucy, a task he takes on with great enthusiasm. As she grows she challenges his knowledge with the myriad questions of childhood, but he answers them without really answering them. When Lucy is seven—the mental age of her father—Sam lovingly plans an elaborate party for her. Unfortunately some parents are unsympathetic to his generous but socially inept efforts and alert Social Services. Prompted also by a picture Lucy has drawn of herself depicting her exaggeratedly large self holding the hand of her father, who is depicted as miniscule, Social

Services takes her away and puts her in a foster home. Sam is devastated. With little social support but that of his mentally retarded friends and the coffee shop owner for whom he works, he goes looking for a lawyer to take his case, determined to get his daughter back.

It is an agonizing situation, because of the profound love he has for his little daughter. The deep emotion that is present, perhaps even visible in every word, speaks of boundless, unceasing love.

Listen to the words of this love poem:

Thirsty deserts will be glad;
Barren lands will celebrate and blossom with flowers.
Deserts will bloom everywhere and sing joyful songs.
They will be as majestic as Mount Lebanon,
    as glorious as Mount Carmel or Sharon Valley.
Everyone will see the wonderful splendor
Of the LORD our God.

Doesn't sound like any love poem you ever heard, does it? But that is what it is. Can you see it? Don't the words of Isaiah come alive for you? What a picture, what a beautiful picture. The parched dryness of the desert badlands is transformed into lush greenness, like the Amazon rainforest. The greens are bright and deep and clear; variations abound like the painter's palette. Flowers blossom in purples and red and yellow and white and pink. And the trees stand tall, poplars and cedars and pine, reaching in adoration to the heavens, showing the majesty and wonder of God. And the heavens rejoice. It is the love of God made manifest, come alive, on earth.

For Isaiah of Jerusalem, the return of the exiles is not simply release from their Babylonian captivity. It is a vision of splendor. It is the revelation of the glory of God in majesty and awe. It is the love of God demonstrated anew as the people of God prepare to embrace new life, new hope, new joy. It is divine love glorious and incomparable, bringing restoration to people whose existence as a people had all but gone. It is renewal to the lost and forgotten, revival to the dead and dying. And it calls them and us to a new understanding of the amazing love of God.

Yes, we are securely in the season of Advent, a time of preparation, and no matter what the scriptures tell us, no matter how much we know that the Anointed One has already come into our midst, we wait. We wait with longing for the new day that the prophet promised the exiles God would bring into being.

The oracles that Isaiah brought to the people of Jerusalem, who, as one commentator names it, were caught in the eye of the Assyrian storm, spoke of destruction. Isaiah warned that the Lord mighty and strong would come like a storm of hail and tempest and overflowing waters. It is a picture not unlike the hurricanes of recent memory to the people of Florida and Louisiana. And these oracles speak to us who, like the people of Jerusalem, have wallowed in the injustice of greed and apathy. We too have become drunk with the pleasures of the affluent that leave the poor lost and weeping for the essentials of life. We have too easily dismissed or become deaf to the cry of the weak, the sick, the abused and oppressed. And we too have sought alliances with earthly powers that totter like iron statues with feet of clay.

But, out of love, God calls to us and strengthens the weak hands, makes firm the feeble knees. Weak hands and minds like Sam's who fear the power structures that seek to deny the sufficiency of his love for his daughter. Be strong, do not fear. God comes to right the wrongs, to repay with saving grace those who have been victimized and demeaned. Where world powers have trod upon hearts and lives, denying the humanity of every person through inhuman servitude and degrading devaluation, God comes to redeem, reclaim, restore, replenish, and renew God's people.

My soul magnifies the Holy One and my spirit rejoices in God my Savior. For God has looked with favor on the lowliness of all God's servants.

Yes, the prophet declares it. God comes with vengeance to save us. God comes with terrible recompense. It is redemption both physical and spiritual, but it is not a call for human vengeance. It is not a call to hate or to bear arms. It is not God's promise to be on our side, the "right" side against those whom we deny the right to their identity, also as children of God. God looks with eyes of love on fallen humanity, on all people, and with a heart of love makes the promise of justice to all people.

Yes, God will come to save us, even from the enemy within ourselves. This little apocalypse of Isaiah is not about vengeance, but about love. It gives us a picture of that time when the ransomed shall rejoice and the glory of God shall be revealed. It speaks of a love that will not let us go, no matter how much we wander. Like Sam in the movie, who, with few financial resources nonetheless got himself the best lawyer possible; like Sam who never gave up his quest to show those in authority that his love was sufficient to meet the real needs of his daughter, God never gives up on us.

God shows us that love, the love of God, the love that God has placed in our hearts, is enough to save a dying world, a world gone mad.

Listen as the poem continues:

The blind will see, and the ears of the deaf will be healed.
Those who were lame will leap around like deer;
Tongues once silent will begin to shout.
Water will rush through the desert.
Scorching sand will turn into a lake,
    and thirsty ground will flow with fountains.
Grass will grow in wetlands,
    where packs of wild dogs once made their home.

Can you picture it? Eyes blinded by fear are opened to the presence of one who, seen with the eyes of faith, never fails. Those who were deaf to the voice of God hear again through the voice of those in need and reach out to help feed a hungry world, to clothe the naked, and to fight for justice for all people. And bent and broken bodies stand tall because with the love of God and neighbor in our hearts, we give beyond the asking. And lives are saved, and rivers of joy flow in hearts where despair once rested. The shadowed landscape of troubled minds now blossoms and blooms with peace and tranquility, and lush grass waves in the breezes of joy, filling the empty spaces and nurturing the once dry places.

It is the love of God shining brightly on the face of the earth, and in the depths of our souls, so that we reach out and embrace each other. Strangers are no more, and "friend" is on the face of everyone we meet.

For the weak have been renewed in strength, the hungry sit at the banquet table, and the glory of God is revealed in the world.

It is a new way, a way of love that bursts forth and makes us open our eyes in wonder. It is a straight way that leads to life, and those who have accepted the redemption that God offers, who have embraced with thanksgiving the love of God in their hearts and shared that love with the poor, the hungry, the naked, the weak, the lost, those ones walk on singing and dancing and shouting. That's the message of this love poem that Isaiah writes to the exiles, to us, in this Advent season.

At the end of the movie, after the powers that be have seen the light and returned Lucy to her father, we see Lucy playing soccer. Sam is the referee and Lucy makes a play and scores a goal. Sam is ecstatic. He picks Lucy up in his arms and with an exuberance of joy he begins to run around the soccer field with her in his arms. The other children begin to run behind him, and the joy that he is experiencing is so palpable, so extravagant, that as you watch you are caught up in it. Unfailingly for me, laughter and tears of joy bubble forth. And for a moment it is like the laughter on that day when Christ comes and with joy takes the righteous in his arms, and joy and gladness overtake the throng. And the ransomed come with singing and rejoicing.

Hear the ending of the poem.

> The people the LORD has rescued
>> will come back with singing as they enter Zion.
> Happiness will be a crown they will always wear.
> They will celebrate and shout
>> because all sorrows and worries will be gone far away.

Oh, it will not be a quiet procession. It will be a homecoming with shouts and waves and hugs and singing and laughter and great joy. That is the promise, that is the assurance, that is the message from the prophet. It is a message of hope, of Advent, of Christ coming into our lives and into our world to redeem the world. And it is all about love.

FOR THE COMMON GOOD

This sermon was preached at the Tuesday Chapel Service at Garrett-Evangelical Theological Seminary.

SCRIPTURE TEXT: 1 Corinthians 12:3b–13

SERMON STYLE: Narrative inductive

GOOD NEWS STATEMENT: The Holy Spirit gifts us for faithful discipleship.

"Tight shoes give you bad eyes." That's what my mother used to say to me. "Tight shoes give you bad eyes." I liked shoes—still do, and I didn't have good sense then not to buy shoes that didn't quite fit, if I really liked the shoe. Oh, I would make sure I could get my feet into it—usually I did that only with sling back shoes, but nevertheless, my feet would hurt in the hot Caribbean weather. And there she would be just waiting to say "Tight shoes give you bad eyes." No, she wasn't an eye specialist, but perhaps she had learned something from this letter that Paul wrote to the Corinthians, the whole portion, not just the piece you heard, but the remaining verses that talk about the parts of the body and the way they work together. I think my mother was privy to a lesson that so many of us Christians need to learn.

It was the lesson that Paul was trying to teach the Corinthians with all the stuff that was going on in the congregation. Corinth seemed like an ideal place to start a church. It was a principal city of the area, a place of great trade; and Paul, the apostle to the Gentiles, found that there was great accommodation for his message. At Corinth both wealthy and poor joined the fledgling Jesus movement and the church began to grow. More than that, the Holy Spirit came upon the church and with great largesse distributed gifts in abundance to the gathered community. There were all kinds of gifts floating around—wisdom, knowledge, faith, healing, working of miracles, prophecy, discernment of spirit, various kinds of tongues, and the interpretation of tongues—to name a few.

Truly, they've got it going on and there is activity all around. Remember in the house churches people are living on site and there are those who are coming and going, doing the work of ministry. Can you see it? Folks are gathering and praying and singing and greeting new converts. And those who have received spiritual gifts are exercising those gifts and they are breaking bread together and sharing their goods with one another and welcoming all in the name of the Lord Jesus. And everything is just as it should be for the beloved community.

Hey, not so fast, Madam Preacher! All is not as well as you make it out to be. There are divisions, cliques in the church. Folks are choosing sides and looking down on other folks because of who baptized them, who is their spiritual father. There are rumors of sexual immorality, and pagan customs are creeping in. And it gets worse: the wealthy are pulling rank; their servants have to prepare the food for the common meal and then clean up, so by the time they arrive, all that's left are the scraps. So the meal has taken on a new meaning—or no meaning at all. But there is an even greater problem. And this one hits at the root of their identity as the church—the gathered community.

You see, it seems as though the Holy Spirit was not very discriminating in her gift-giving. She kind of just reached into her gift bag and handed out gifts willy-nilly. No, that's not what happened? You mean I got it wrong? So you're saying she chose special people to give those special gifts? And since the birthing gift was tongues, everyone knows that's the best gift in the church—so only special people got that and they should be recognized, shouldn't they?

No? Well that's what they told me when I stopped by to visit at that church and I didn't have that gift, so of course I was treated with scant courtesy. Why wasn't I chosen? My gift is hospitality and I think I have a little wisdom too. So why isn't my gift the same as theirs? Those are the questions that Paul is trying to answer, questions that are still plaguing the church today. The gift of choice has changed, and these days it is not even spiritual gifts that are honored the most. Generally honor is given to those who can give great financial gifts to the church. The big givers at every level act and are treated as though they are special because of their ability to give a lot of money.

In Corinth it was spiritual gifts that gave those Corinthians a feeling of privilege. You see, they missed the purpose of the gifts that they had been given. They thought that their spiritual gifts, especially the gift of speaking in tongues, were extra-special, and that those gifts made them special, better than everyone else. But they missed the point. The Holy Spirit as the giver of all gifts in the church determines to whom the gifts are given. Every gift is given by the same Spirit and every gift has equal value; none is better than another; but more than that, each gift is given for the same reason.

Have you ever wondered why you are able to do a particular thing and not another? Have you ever tried to operate from a position that you had no idea about or, more to the point, that you are a total dud at doing? And then, you woke up and did exactly what God had gifted you to do—what a difference! It's like someone who is color blind trying to be an interior decorator or someone who doesn't know how to boil water deciding to make a seven-course dinner for a dozen visiting dignitaries.

Paul writes that there are varieties of gifts, but the same Spirit. On the day of Pentecost, if we really pay attention to the text, the gift of tongues was given so that the people who were present could understand what was being said. Do you get it? The disciples were all Galileans, but not so the people who crowded the Jerusalem streets to celebrate the harvest. Yet each person there heard the message of Christ in his or her own language. The Holy Spirit knew that was what was needed for that moment. The Holy Spirit, the author of all spiritual gifts, provided the gift that was needed for the common good.

Yes, that's the message. That's what Paul wanted the Corinthians to understand about the gifts of the Holy Spirit. Each got not only what was needed to do the work of Christ, not only according to each one's ability, but what the body needed to be complete. Each gift that was given was to be exercised for the good of all, for the common good. Each was part of a whole and the ministry of the one was for the benefit of the whole. The work of the one, the experience of the one, the ministry of the one, was for the sake, the benefit, the blessing of all— for the good of all.

It is like the body that needs all its parts, that does not operate as well when one of its parts is in pain. Tight shoes give you bad eyes. My mother knew what she was talking about. She knew that the pain in my feet would affect my whole body, even my eyes, and she was right. Oh, she didn't have the eloquence of Paul, but the message was the same, and it is still the same today. Each of us is part and parcel of everyone else. In the church each of us is given the gifts that we have been given for the good of everyone else. We are together the body of Christ, and each of us has a function in the body. We have all been baptized into that one body, and our participation in the body helps to make it healthy or to make it sick. The gifts that we have received serve the purpose of building up the body. Individually we are all members of the body of Christ, and the gifts of the Spirit that we have received enable us to live together under the one head, Jesus Christ.

So what are the gifts that you have received from Christ? Have you taken stock lately? No? Perhaps you should, because the body cannot function completely without your gift. Or perhaps you don't know what your particular gift is or gifts are? Well it's time you found out because the body needs you. Or worse yet, perhaps you've been hiding your gift or using it only for yourself or for those special people in your life. Well, if you have, give it up, bring it here. The Holy Spirit gave it to you for the sake of the body of Christ. The Holy Spirit gifts us for faithful discipleship.

Listen again to what Paul says, "To each is given the manifestation of the Spirit for the common good." That is the reason that you have been called and gifted by our gracious God. And we are all waiting to share in the benefit and the joy that your gifts have to offer to the whole people of God, to the church, the body of Christ. The Holy Spirit gifts each of us for the benefit of all. So come bring your gifts and allow them to take their place in building up the body of Christ, and let us all experience the goodness of God through you.

LIFE-GIVING BREAD

This sermon was preached to the Christ UMC and Mount Greenwood UMC in Illinois at a Sunday service.

SCRIPTURE TEXT: John 6:51–58

SERMON STYLE: Narrative deductive

GOOD NEWS STATEMENT: Jesus nourishes us for living.

Have you ever baked your own bread from scratch? Or perhaps you have bought refrigerated dough and baked it at home. Well, if you have, perhaps you remember the smell of baking bread—actually the smell of the yeast—and how it made you hungry to taste the bread hot out of the oven. I can make all kinds of bread. I learned from watching both my mother and father, but I don't make it too often because I love bread too much!

As a child we made bread every week; where I grew up most large families did. I would watch as my mother or my father poured out the flour in a special kneading tray, then added a little sugar, salt, butter, lard, and then the yeast that had been set to rise. Then they would knead all the ingredients, adding warm water until the dough was smooth. Then they would grease the outside of the dough, cover it, and leave it to rise. And that was where the fascination about baking bread came in for me.

I would come back often and watch as the dough began to rise. Sometimes it rose so high that the cloth could no longer cover all the dough and the sides would become exposed. It seemed to me that the dough had a life of its own, that it was alive, and that it was trying to stand up and walk out of the tray. In a sense as it rose then, and again when it was rolled out into loaves and put to cook in the heat of the oven, that dough was alive. It was living bread.

Our Gospel lesson for today, John 6:51–58, is a continuation of the texts from the last three weeks. Step back with me for a moment to the beginning of chapter 6. In the first part of the chapter, Jesus feeds the five thousand gathered on the hillside with bread and fish. It is a miracle feeding because he uses a small gift of five loaves and two fish to satisfy the hunger of five thousand men plus women and children, and had enough leftovers to fill twelve baskets! Because of the miracle, the people begin to acknowledge his identity as Messiah, or as John 6:14 records it, "the prophet who is to come into the world." And they want to make him king, but Jesus knows that his status and his stature come from God alone, and so he goes away; but the crowds follow.

The crowds, like the paparazzi that follow today's movie stars, will not leave Jesus alone. They follow him. They are impressed by the miracle. They want more. They want more signs. They want more bread. And Jesus says to them, I am the only bread you need for your life. In fact, I am life-giving bread. This human bread that filled your stomachs, like the manna, the bread of heaven that your ancestors received in the wilderness, is earthly bread. It is bread that does not last, that is only for the time it takes for the body to ingest it, to keep the nutrients it needs, and to discard the rest. What I offer you is not temporal bread, it is eternal bread, heavenly food. "I am the bread of life." "I am the living bread that came down from heaven."

As Christians and disciples of Jesus Christ, when we hear those words our hearts rejoice. We believe in Jesus Christ as the Son of God and Savior of the world, and so we look to Jesus to fill our lives with love, to give us the grace we need to make it through all the changing scenes of life. But that was not the way Jesus' audience heard his words; for them this was a startling, almost blasphemous statement. For the listening audience, the first two words of Jesus' declaration held great significance. If you know the story of Moses and the burning bush, you may remember that when Moses questioned the identity of the voice that spoke to him, the response was "I AM." Moses asked: "Who shall I tell the people sent me to you?" And Exodus 3:14 records: "God said to Moses, 'I AM WHO I AM. . . . Thus you shall say to the Israelites, "I AM has sent me to you."'" And from that time forward the people of Israel understood those two small words "I AM" to represent God. So perhaps you can begin to understand the consternation of the people when Jesus uses the term I AM to refer to himself. Would you not be perturbed, even upset, if someone that you knew as a regular person told you that he or she was God? Yes, we understand Jesus as the Son of God, but they did not—not yet.

And Jesus does not stop there. He says, I AM the bread of heaven, you must eat of my flesh. Sounds like cannibalism, doesn't it? In fact, the early Christians were accused of cannibalism because of this very statement about eating flesh. And so Jesus' hearers ask: "How can this man give us his flesh to eat?" It is a natural question for persons who do not understand the sacrifice that Jesus Christ made of himself for all of us. And remember also that at this point Jesus has not yet suffered death, been resurrected, or ascended. So these first hearers cannot be faulted because they do not understand what Jesus is saying.

The writer of the Gospel of John, himself a Jewish Christian, is addressing his text to a Jewish Christian community that is in conflict. Bible historians tell us that the conflict was mainly between the synagogue authorities—generally the Pharisees—and these Christians who believe in Jesus as the promised Messiah. John wants to prove that Jesus is indeed Messiah and God and that their lives are dependent on their belief in Jesus the Christ; that only by believing in Jesus, only by accepting Jesus into one's being, by eating his flesh and drinking his blood, can anyone live. Their tradition of Judaism stretched back in time for many generations, and at the time of the writing of this gospel, Jesus' resurrection and ascension was only about fifty to seventy years old. So it is difficult for everyone to accept. They, like so many of us, had problems with change. I am sure that most if not all of you understand what I am saying, especially at this time in the first few weeks of having a new pastor. Things have changed, things are no longer quite as you are used to them, and it does not feel right. Even if the change is for the better, it is hard to take because it is not what you have been accustomed to. The message of Jesus was as new to them as your new pastor is to you, and it was as hard for them to trust his words as it is for some of you to trust Pastor Jacqueline. Faith in Jesus as the Son of God was a hard change for many to accommodate.

Jesus says, "I am the living bread." There is something about living things; anything that is living moves. Living things do not stay the same way all the time. Living things—you and I, churches that are alive—move and change. And Jesus says, if your life comes from me, if what makes you alive is what you get from me, if you eat the bread that is my body, you will have life. If you eat this life-giving bread that I AM, then and only then will you have eternal life. And isn't that the whole purpose of our lives as Christians? The hope that we all have is that we will receive new life through Jesus Christ in this world, so that we can live eternally with God, and we can do that only if we partake of the living bread.

As you hear this you might think it refers to the sacrament of Holy Communion, and you would be correct, but only partly. Because even if you partook of the sacrament as often as John Wesley advised us, even if you took communion every day, that alone would be insufficient to ensure your eternal life. It is not the bread and the wine, representatives of Jesus' body and blood, that give you life. It is Christ who enables you to ensure your eternity with God. You must eat Christ, the living bread that changes our human nature and brings it closer to the divine. You must partake of the living, life-giving bread by enabling Jesus Christ to fill you with grace so that you can live the life of love that only his presence can give. You must allow Jesus Christ to fill your whole being, so that you can experience the change of heart that his presence living in each of us gives. Jesus said: "Those who eat my flesh and drink my blood abide in me and I in them. Just as the living Father sent me, and I live because of the Father, so whoever eats me will live because of me." What Jesus is saying to each of us today and every day of our lives is that we cannot be content with being just as we are, with doing things just as we have always done, with remaining the same as though Jesus is not the foundation of our Christian lives.

No! Jesus calls us to receive his Spirit within our spirit so that we can live in unity with him. Jesus calls us to love as he loves; to receive one another not as strangers or newcomers, but as friends. And the beauty of it all is that Jesus does not ask us to do all this on our own. No! Jesus not only invites us to live with God as he did, but Jesus gives us all that we need in order to live the life that ensures us eternal life. Jesus offers us himself freely. Jesus gives us himself, his flesh, his body, and his blood, his life sacrificed for us, his assurance bought for us, his love, never-ending for us. That is the living bread.

On those Saturdays of my childhood when the bread came out hot from the oven, my mother or my father would cut each of us a large slice, put butter on it, and hand it over. Our faces, soon to be greasy with the dripping butter, would light up as we relished the taste of that fresh warm bread on our tongues and in our mouths. And as I took the first bite, I would close my eyes in appreciation and joy. Well, I'm here to tell you that as great as that experience was, and as much as it still brings me joy to eat freshly baked bread, it is nothing compared to the joy that awaits us when we eat of the life-giving bread that is Jesus Christ. The joy that we feel comes from the knowledge that we have new life. Our lives depend on this bread; our lives depend on Jesus; and ecstatic joy is ours, all of ours, when we feast on Christ in this life and when in that eternal kingdom we feast forever at his banquet table.

Today, right now, Jesus calls you, calls each of us to come and taste and see the body of our Lord, to drink the wine of heaven that is his blood. It is free to all who desire it. Jesus is the living bread, come down from heaven for you, for me, giving new life to all who desire to be with him eternally. Come eat the living bread, Jesus Christ, the word made flesh. Eat and live forevermore.

LIVING INTO THE PROMISES

This sermon was preached to the staff of the General Board of Pensions of the United Methodist Church.

SCRIPTURE TEXT: Isaiah 43:18–25

SERMON STYLE: Topical sermon that makes points

GOOD NEWS STATEMENT: God empowers us for faithful living.

> God of our weary years, God of our silent tears
> Thou who has brought us thus far on the way;
> Thou who hast by thy might led us into the light,
> Keep us forever in the path we pray.
> Lest our feet stray from the places, our God, where we met thee;
> Lest our hearts drunk with the wine of the world, we forget thee;
> Shadowed beneath thy hand may we forever stand
> True to our God, true to our native land.

The words have become so familiar to so many of us in the African-American community that we sing it with the gusto of celebration and triumph, rather than with the solemnity and prayerful devotion it really requires. If ever there was a prayer for strength, if ever there was a prayer for God's sustaining grace, if ever there was an appeal from a people who knew that they needed God, this is it.

I remember the first time I heard this hymn. I was at an event in New York. It was a dinner given by the Urban League of New York

City, and my white friend and I, both managers, had been sent as representatives of our company. It was an early evening affair and we had gone shopping first. We arrived just as they were about to start and hurriedly found our place. Tired from all the running around, we sat down to rest our weary feet.

We were far from the stage anyway, so when they announced the "song" and people stood up and began to sing, we decided to stay seated. After about thirty seconds into the song, a sister—I can only call her that for her kindness—leaned over to me and said, "You really should stand, this is the Negro National Anthem." I jumped to my feet, leaned over to my friend and said, "Stand up." She did. Then I told the sister, "I did not know." She replied kindly, "I thought so. That is why I told you."

It was never the same for me again. I quickly learned the words of that great prayer hymn and as I did I came to see it as a desire on the part of a people to live into the promises of God. It is a song that the Hebrew people could have sung during their sojourn in the wilderness as they tried to reach the promised land. It is a song that the Israelites to whom Isaiah is speaking in this passage could have sung as they contemplated the word brought by Second Isaiah that their warfare had ended, that deliverance and restoration was on the way, that they would soon be going home.

The situation of this text is that the people of Israel have not yet returned home, they have not yet ended their time of exile, but the former things, their submission to the Babylonian Empire, is at an end. Babylon has been overthrown and there's a new sheriff in town. Persia is in the ascendancy and the people have received a message from God—it is a word of promise and the prophet calls them to begin to live into the promise, to keep their faith in Yahweh. More than that, they are encouraged to remain steadfast and to believe that God who keeps covenant has not left them, will not leave them. God's promise is sure and God will deliver on God's promises. That's a message for us as well: God delivers on God's promises.

"Do not remember the former things, or consider the things of old." Somehow this seems to fly in the face of popular wisdom that says, "Those who ignore the past are doomed to repeat it." So if you believe that is true, and I do, what do we make of this passage? How do we accommodate it in our living as people of promise—because that's who we are as Christians? And since this is Black History Month, it is requisite that I say also, that's who we are as black people in America. So how do we live today forgetting the former things?

Old Testament scholars tell us that the former things of which Second Isaiah spoke included the record of God's coming judgment, of the pending exile at the hands of the Babylonians, and the message in this text from Isaiah 43 is that God, who has redeemed God's people, has moved on from the stance of judgment and is now showering mercy and blessings in abundance. Isn't that just like our God? But, you see, that's not the whole of the message, and if we want to appropriate it for our context, our postresurrection context as Christians, and our postsixties–civil rights struggle as African Americans, we cannot, we must not stop there. We must hear the rest of the prophet's message from God:

> Do not remember the former things, or consider the things of old. I am about to do a new thing; now it springs forth, do you not perceive it? (Isa. 43:18–19)

God says forget about looking back at the past. It's over. It's gone. There's a new day coming. I, Yahweh, the God of covenant, I am about to do a new thing. The message continues: Because of God's promises we can let go of the past.

In his chronicle of the civil rights struggle in America entitled *Martin & Malcolm & America: A Dream or a Nightmare,* James Cone juxtaposes Dr. King's and Malcolm X's expectations regarding America's response to the passage of the civil rights bill. Where Dr. King believed optimistically that whites in America would live into the promise of freedom and equality for all people, Malcolm had no confidence in that belief ever becoming a reality. Cone writes:

> In contrast to Malcolm's views, Martin believed in whites because he believed in the goodness of humanity. He believed in humanity because he believed in God, the One who created male and female in the image and likeness of the divine.[1]

And I submit to you that despite what happened later, despite his assassination, Dr. King was right. He chose to live into the promise of God, that in Christ we are all equal. We are no longer black or white, slave or free, rich or poor. We are all one in Christ Jesus. And as Christians we are called to live into that promise that God has made, to live into the covenant that God has already kept through the death and resurrection of Jesus Christ. But how do we do that?

When we look around, we are still black and white in America. We are still slave and free, caught in the traps that have been laid for us by our conforming to the world's standards and mores instead of allowing our minds to be renewed in Christ Jesus. We are more than ever rich and poor, not just around the world in nations whose suffering, whose demise from poverty and years of oppression barely, if ever, get a mention on the nightly news because it is so commonplace (it's not sexy), not just in Africa and Asia, but right here in America as Katrina so clearly showed us by blowing off the covers of our secret sins.

How do we live into the promises in the face of our own sins, our individual sins, the sins of our society, our world, and to our shame, our church, the systems that guide and even control us? How do we live past all that "stuff?" Isaiah tells us. Through the prophet's mouth God says to us: "you have burdened me with your sins; you have wearied me with your iniquities. I am he who blots out your transgressions for my own sake, and I will not remember your sins."

Did you hear that? Not for any good that we have done. By grace we have been saved through faith and it is not of our own doing. No, it is the gift of God. That is the message of this Isaiah text for us. That is the promise that must guide our lives. God gifts us with grace to live into the promises of God, to live faithfully as Christians. It is the only way that we can live as children of God, sojourners who live on earth as kingdom dwellers. It takes faith in God's promises, but did God not already come through by sending Jesus to take the heat for our sins? Through Jesus we have become a new creation. God has already done it, so all we have to do is praise God and live into it.

God is always doing a new thing. So, forgetting what lies behind, we ought to press on; we ought to live into the promise that God has made to us through Jesus Christ. Oh, we must not forget the struggles that brought us even thus far, and, yes, we have a long way to go. None of us, black or white, Christians all, have arrived at the place where we ought to be. God is not finished with us yet. And as African Americans we must not allow ourselves to be caught up in the myth that we have arrived, we have made it—or at least that some of us have. The reality is that if not all have made it, none have made it. So we must press on, keep marching, keep praying, keep standing, keep walking, keep talking, keep singing, keep believing, keep praising God for what God has done and what God is doing with us. God is still leading us to the place of everlasting promise, and by God's gift of grace, by faith, we can live into that promise.

And living into God's promise, we can be the new thing that God is doing in the world; we can be the people that can offer our praise by showing God's love in the world. God fulfills God's promise in us. So let us live in the assurance of God's everlasting love. And with God's love in us, we can live faithfully as Christians, showing God's love in the world. For shadowed beneath God's hand we can forever stand true to our God, because we are standing on the promises of God.

Thanks be to God.

APPENDIX A:
Guidelines for Homiletical Exegesis for Good News Sermons

A. IDENTIFYING THE GOOD NEWS

- Approach the text or topic with prayerful expectation of finding good news.
- Find the theological meaning: What does the text or topic say about God and the divine/human relationship?
- Name the good news: Identify the divine action that speaks of human transformation.
- Identify a charge to the hearers that is fueled by the good news.

B. INTERPRETING THE BIBLICAL TEXT OR THE TOPIC

- Meet the text or topic: Approach with the intention of uncovering good news.
- Establish the boundaries of the text: Is there special significance to its placement? Are there bridge words that move the message of the text?
- Locate the text historically: What is the historical setting, that is, the social, religious, cultural, (etc.) realities that confront or are confronted by the text in its original setting? How did the text function in and affect the lives of those who heard it first?

- Identify the literary form of the text and its influence on the reading of the text. Does the form offer a model for the sermon?
- Consider the theological implications of the text: What is its influence on Christian doctrine or practice? How is it supported biblically?
- Connect text and topic and identify biblical and theological agreements or differences.

C. ANALYSIS OF THE CONTEXT

- Approach the situation of preaching with the understanding that the congregation has the expectation of hearing good news.
- What is the congregational context in which the sermon will be preached? What are the social, cultural, theological, and doctrinal norms?
- Establish the boundaries of the preaching context: liturgical or social implications, societal or world events.
- Connect context with text: Is there special significance to the context that has implications for the meaning of the text?
- Determine the appropriateness of the good news: How can the message of the text be transformative for the individual hearers or for the congregation?

APPENDIX B:
Questions for Homiletical Exegesis
of a Biblical Text

A. MEETING THE TEXT

- Does the preacher approach the text with expectation of hearing something new?
- Have you heard the text, that is, engaged your sense of hearing deliberately?
- What does the text offer given multiple and different emphases?
- What initial impressions, questions, and sermon ideas come to mind?
- What is the good news in the text?

B. ESTABLISHING THE BOUNDARIES OF THE TEXT

- What is its placement in the corpus?
- What is the level of authorship—historical event, oral tradition, or redactor?
- Is there special significance to its placement?
- How is this passage used in the context of the corpus?

C. LOCATING THE TEXT HISTORICALLY

- What is the historical setting and how much of it does your sermon require?

- Who was the author of the text?
- Where and when was the text written?
- Why or for what situation was the text written?
- What are the social, religious, and cultural realities of the text in its original setting?
- How did it function in and affect the lives of those who heard it first?

D. IDENTIFYING THE FORM OF THE TEXT AND ITS INFLUENCE ON THE READING OF THE TEXT

- What is the literary form of the text?
- What are the bridge words that move the message of the text?
- Which words have history that bears examination?
- Does the literary form offer a model for the sermon?

E. MEETING THE CONGREGATION

- What is the congregation's expectation of hearing good news?
- What is the social, cultural, theological, and doctrinal situation of the congregation?
- What is the congregational context in which the sermon will be preached?

F. ESTABLISHING THE BOUNDARIES OF THE PREACHING CONTEXT

- What is the situation of the preaching moment?
- Does the liturgical season have relevance for the preaching context?
- Are there societal or world events that would influence the content of the sermon?

G. SIGNIFICANCE OF THE TEXT FOR THE PRESENT

- Are there parallels between the text and the current situation of the congregation?
- How does this text achieve significance for the present congregation?

- How much of the historical atmosphere and feeling does the congregation need to experience imaginatively for the text to operate at the highest level?
- Which words have greatest (and least) relevance for the present reality?

H. CONNECTING THE CONTEXT OF THE CONGREGATION WITH THE TEXT

- What in the text may offend or challenge, instruct or affirm the hearers?
- What would be the immediate reaction or response to the text?
- How is the good news that arises from the text significant for this congregation?
- How can the message of the text be transformative for the congregation?
- Is there an obvious discipleship message in the text?

APPENDIX C:
Questions for Homiletical Exegesis of a Topic

A. MEETING THE TOPIC
- What general topic are you addressing?
- What is the content of the good news that the topic offers?
- What discipleship message arises from this topic?

B. ESTABLISHING THE BOUNDARIES OF THE TOPIC
- Which aspect of the general topic, for example, the particular subtopic, will the sermon consider?
- In this topic representative of a particular Christian doctrine or practice?
- What is the particular scope you are addressing in the sermon?
- What are the key points for preaching that exposes the topic to the congregation?
- Is the topic congruent with Christian doctrine or practice?

C. CONNECTING THE TOPIC WITH SCRIPTURE
- Is there a biblical foundation that supports this topic?
- Did the topic originate from a specific text?
  - If yes, have you done biblical interpretation on that text?

- ◆ If no, what text would provide a foundation for the topic and what other texts would provide supportive material?
- ▪ What scripture texts have other preachers used to address this topic?

D. Locating the Topic Theologically and Doctrinally

- ▪ How has the topic been understood and interpreted theologically?
- ▪ Is the subject of the topic in accord with accepted Christian doctrines?
- ▪ Is the topic in accordance with Christian or denominational tradition?
- ▪ Does the approach fit the doctrinal understanding of the congregation?

E. Locating the Topic Historically and Contextually

- ▪ How has this topic been approached historically in the congregation and in the wider church?
- ▪ What, if any, misunderstandings has the preaching of this topic caused previously?
- ▪ Is the text appropriate for the theological and denominational beliefs of the congregation?
- ▪ Is there a situation present in the society or the world for which this topic has particular relevance?

F. Meeting the Congregation

- ▪ What does this topic say to or about this congregation?
- ▪ Is there a reason or situation past or present why the congregation will resist hearing this topic preached?
- ▪ Does the presentation of the topic lend itself to offering good news to the hearers?

G. Establishing the Boundaries of the Preaching Context

- ▪ What is the congregation's expectation of hearing good news?
- ▪ What is the social, cultural, theological, and doctrinal situation of the congregation?

- What is the congregational context in which the sermon will be preached?
- What is the situation of the preaching moment?
- Does the liturgical season have relevance for the preaching context?
- Are there societal or world events that would influence the content of the sermon?

H. SIGNIFICANCE OF THE TOPIC FOR THE PRESENT

- Why does this topic achieve significance for the present situation of individuals or the whole congregation?
- Which aspect of the topic has greatest (and least) relevance for the present reality?
- Do the good news and the message of the sermon fit the topic?

APPENDIX D:
Weekly Schedule for Sermon Preparation

MONDAY: READ THE TEXT

- Read the chosen scripture text as part of your early morning devotions.
- Read the full pericope and surrounding text as you are led in your reading.
- Listen carefully for the message of divine grace that arises from the text.

TUESDAY: IDENTIFY THE GOOD NEWS AND THE MESSAGE OF THE SERMON, THEN BEGIN EXEGESIS

- Read the text as part of your morning devotions.
- Begin the initial work of interpretation through research and data gathering.
- Develop good news and message statements.

WEDNESDAY: FRAME THE SERMON

- Complete the research and any remaining exegetical work.
- Develop an outline based on the style or intended shape of the sermon.

THURSDAY: PREPARE THE SERMON MANUSCRIPT

- Complete the outline.
- Create the sermon manuscript.
- Verify or modify the good news and message statements in the manuscript.
- Allow the material of the sermon to permeate the mind and the heart.

FRIDAY: READ, REVIEW, REVISE, REFORMULATE

- Read the manuscript carefully, engaging all your senses in verifying its contents.
- Review the contents with respect to text or topic and preaching context.
- Pay special attention to transitions between the major sections and functionality of the introduction and conclusion.
- Make revisions and practice reading the sermon aloud, preferably before a mirror.
- Create notes for preaching (if applicable).

SATURDAY: REREAD, ABSORB THE MESSAGE, AND RELAX

- Review all aspects of the sermon.
- Practice preaching the sermon (before a mirror adds value to the exercise).
- Relax and allow the message to take root.

SUNDAY: PREACH THE SERMON AND LET IT GO

- Saturate the sermon in prayer.
- Leave room for the Holy Spirit.
- Preach the sermon.
- Let it go—avoid rehashing.
- Relax.

APPENDIX E:
Preaching Feedback Form

Did you hear good news in this sermon?   ☐ Yes ☐ No

What was it? _____

_____

_____

Did you hear a distinct message from this sermon?   ☐ Yes ☐ No

What was it? _____

_____

_____

Did you hear anything that related to your discipleship? ☐ Yes ☐ No

What was it? _____

_____

_____

Did the scriptures come through clearly? ☐ Yes ☐ No

Which passage(s)? _____

_____

_____

Did this sermon tell you anything about God? ☐ Yes ☐ No

What was it? _____

_____

_____

Did the sermon hold your attention? ☐ Yes ☐ No

If yes, how? If no, why not? _____

_____

_____

Did this sermon relate well to this congregation? ☐ Yes ☐ No

Why or why not? _____

_____

_____

NOTES

PREFACE

1. Samuel D. Proctor, *The Certain Sound of the Trumpet: Crafting a Sermon of Authority* (Valley Forge, Pa.: Judson Press, 1994), 12.

2. Ronald J. Allen, *Preaching: An Essential Guide* (Nashville: Abingdon Press, 2002), 20. Allen devotes his first chapter to the subject of good news as it arises from the text and is interpreted as the Word of God. He addresses the subject further in his treatment of contextualizing the sermon for the congregation.

CHAPTER ONE

1. Marjorie Hewitt Suchocki, *The Whispered Word: A Theology of Preaching* (St. Louis: Chalice Press, 1999), 2. Suchocki is a process theologian, who recognizes God as "everlastingly creative, continually calling existence into being through an evocative word."

2. Although the phrase "going on to perfection" has been attributed to the theology of John Wesley, Paul's letter to the Philippians (3:14) offers these sentiments, even more definitively, of continual striving to reach the goal of becoming like Christ.

3. Wesley's preventing grace is more commonly referred to as prevenient grace. It is defined as grace that runs ahead of our desires.

4. Allen, *Preaching: An Essential Guide*, 21. Allen suggests that the preacher summarize the main idea of the sermon with God as subject, the activity of God as the verb, and the predicate as the result of God's re-

deeming activity. He believes that "by making God the subject of this sentence, and the subject of the sermon, preachers remind themselves and the congregation of the centrality of God in the Christian worldview, and of the fact that God's gracious initiatives make possible (and call forth) human response."

5. Edmund A. Steimle, Morris J. Niedenthal, and Charles L. Rice, *Preaching the Story* (Philadelphia: Fortress Press, 1980), 38.

6. Ibid.

7. David Buttrick, *Homiletics: Moves and Structures* (Philadelphia: Fortress Press, 1987), 451.

8. Fred B. Craddock, *Preaching* (Nashville: Abingdon Press, 1985), 51–52.

9. Suchocki, *The Whispered Word*, 4.

10. Suchocki warns that the whispered word of God, always a creative word, "can be drowned out by the sheer weight of the past with which and through which it must work (6) [and is] not always clearly discerned" (13).

11. James Forbes, *The Holy Spirit & Preaching* (Nashville: Abingdon Press, 1989), 19.

12. Ibid., 26.

13. Frank A. Thomas, *They Like to Never Quit Praisin' God: The Role of Celebration in Preaching* (Cleveland: Pilgrim Press, 1997). Thomas' work was a continuation of Henry H. Mitchell's thesis developed in his textbook *Celebration & Experience in Preaching* (Nashville: Abingdon Press, 1990).

14. Ibid., 23.

CHAPTER TWO

1. Eugene L. Lowry, *The Sermon: Dancing the Edge of Mystery* (Nashville: Abingdon Press, 1997), 37.

2. John S. McClure, *Preaching Words: 144 Key Terms in Homiletics* (Louisville: Westminster John Knox Press, 2007), 30–31.

3. Ronald J. Allen, *Preaching the Topical Sermon* (Louisville: Westminster John Knox Press, 1992), 35. In chapter 2, Allen lists several occasions and associated conditions connected with preaching the topical sermon.

4. Ronald J. Allen, *Contemporary Biblical Interpretation for Preaching* (Valley Forge, Pa.: Judson Press, 1984), 3. Allen considers the knowledge of the history of the text as facilitating the emergence of the "ancient dimensions of meaning which are not obvious to the modern eye."

5. Allen, *Preaching: An Essential Guide*, 30.

6. Much of the following descriptive material on these interpretive methods was paraphrased and simplified from various articles about biblical hermeneutics, biblical exegesis, and biblical criticism, including defintions provided by www.wikipedia.com.

7. Most of this interpretive material is taken from: *The New Interpreter's Bible: A Commentary in Twelve Volumes* (Nashville: Abingdon Press, 1994–1998.)

8. For more detailed information on biblical exegesis in connection with preaching, in addition to the text referenced previously in this chapter, see Ronald J. Allen, *Interpreting the Gospel* (St. Louis: Chalice Press, 1998); Thomas G. Long, *Preaching and the Literary Forms of the Bible* (Philadelphia: Fortress Press, 1989); David L. Bartlett, *Between the Bible and the Church: New Methods for Biblical Preaching* (Nashville: Abingdon Press, 1999).

CHAPTER THREE

1. John Vincent directed the Sheffield Inner City Ecumenical Mission and the Urban Theology Unit in Sheffield, England. His book *Into the City* (London: Epworth Press, 1982) "tells of the successes and failures of a group of churches and their members who actually live in the inner city, continuing a Christian witness in old and often unsuitable buildings, working alongside underprivileged immigrants and unemployed in areas whose needs have been ignored and forgotten."

2. Fred B. Craddock, *As One without Authority* (St. Louis: Chalice Press, 2001), 18.

3. Paul Scott Wilson, "Theological Reasons for a Change," in *The Four Pages of the Sermon: A Guide to Biblical Preaching* (Nashville: Abingdon Press, 1999), 20–25. Wilson's Four Page model presents the sermon as four theological pages, two of which present the text as stated in scripture; he connects the biblical record with the preaching context through two parallel theological pages.

4. Ibid., 20.

5. From Paul Scott Wilson, "Biblical Studies and Preaching: A Growing Divide?" in Thomas G. Long and Edward Farley, eds., *Preaching as a Theological Task: World Gospel, Scripture. In Honor of David Buttrick* (Louisville: Westminster John Knox Press, 1996), 137. In this book, fifteen

homileticians/theologians pay homage by addressing a topic of interest or concern to Buttrick. Wilson's offering addresses specifically the connection between theology and scripture.

6. Ibid., 139. The problem is one that Wilson considers to have been inherited from an older model of preaching that does not fit the present.

CHAPTER FOUR

1. O. Wesley Allen, *The Homiletic of ALL Believers: A Conversational Approach* (Louisville: Westminster John Knox Press, 2005), 17. Allen expounds on the requirements and the difficulties of engaging and maintaining these conversations over time, but stresses their importance in the life of the church. He has developed a Matrix of Conversations, which consists of six levels of conversation with the pulpit at the center of the highest level, overlaid on the liturgical conversation that sits on the simultaneous sociohistorical, personal, theological, and congregational conversations.

2. Thomas, *They Like to Never Quit Praisin' God*, 3.

3. Suchocki, *The Whispered Word*, 3. In the language of the process theologian, God is constantly calling all worlds into being through the never ending Word of God. "To exist is, by definition, to be receiving a word from God."

CHAPTER FIVE

1. For descriptions and examples of thirty-four different types of sermons, see Ronald J. Allen, *Patterns of Preaching: A Sermon Sampler* (St. Louis: Chalice Press, 1998).

2. Ibid., 7–13. A description of the Puritan Plain Style and a sample sermon can be found in Allen's text.

3. The Four Pages of the Sermon is a style of sermon developed by Paul Scott Wilson and is explained in a textbook by the same name (Nashville: Abingdon Press, 1999). Wilson considers this style appropriate for all biblical (expository) sermons.

4. Long, *Preaching and the Literary Forms of the Bible*, 138–48. Long provides an extensive description and several examples of this process of developing the outline of the sermon.

5. Ibid.

6. Eugene Lowry, *The Sermon: Dancing the Edge of Mystery* (Nashville: Abingdon Press, 1997), 23.

7. Thomas, *They Like to Never Quit Praisin' God*, 87–89. Thomas charts a process that moves from "Intuitive Complication" through "Intuitive Gospel Assurance" to "Intuitive Celebration," which works as an influence on the emotive behavior of the congregation.

8. Ibid., 88.

CHAPTER SIX

1. Thomas G. Long, in *God's Word and Our Words: Basic Homiletics* by Ronald E. Sleeth (Atlanta: John Knox Press, 1986), vii.

2. Ronald E. Sleeth, *God's Word and Our Words: Basic Homiletics* (Atlanta: John Knox Press, 1986), 7.

3. Lucy Lind Hogan, *Graceful Speech: An Invitation to Preaching* (Louisville: Westminster John Knox Press, 2006), 147.

4. Lucy Atkinson Rose, *Sharing the Word: Preaching in the Roundtable Church* (Louisville: Westminster John Knox Press, 1997), iii. Rose points out that "in conversational views of preaching, sermonic forms seek to engage the community of faith in its central, ongoing conversations."

5. O. Wesley Allen Jr., *The Homiletic of ALL Believers*, 13.

6. Suchocki, *The Whispered Word*, 4.

7. Richard Lischer, "Preaching as the Church's Language," in *Listening to the Word*, edited by Gail R. O'Day and Thomas G. Long (Nashville: Abingdon Press, 1993), 125.

8. Suchocki, *The Whispered Word*, 11.

9. Charles Rice, *The Embodied Word: Preaching as Art and Liturgy* (Minneapolis: Augsburg Fortress, 1991), 51.

10. Ibid., 25.

FOUR SERMONS

1. James Cone, *Martin & Malcolm & America: A Dream or a Nightmare?* (Maryknoll, N.Y.: Orbis Books, 1992), 220.

BIBLIOGRAPHY

Aden, LeRoy H., and Robert G. Hughes. *Preaching God's Compassion.* Minneapolis: Fortress Press, 2002.

Allen, O. Wesley. *The Homiletic of ALL Believers: A Conversational Approach.* Louisville: Westminster John Knox Press, 2005.

Allen, Ronald J. *Contemporary Biblical Interpretation for Preaching.* Valley Forge, Pa.: Judson Press, 1984.

_____ . *Hearing the Sermon: Relationship/Content/Feeling.* St. Louis: Chalice Press, 2004.

_____ . *Interpreting the Gospel.* St. Louis: Chalice Press, 1998.

_____ . *Preaching: An Essential Guide.* (Nashville: Abingdon Press, 2002.

_____ . *Preaching the Topical Sermon.* Louisville: Westminster John Knox Press, 1992.

_____ . *Thinking Theologically.* Minneapolis: Fortress Press, 2008

Allen, Ronald J., and Gilbert L. Bartholomew. *Preaching Verse by Verse.* Louisville: Westminster John Knox Press, 2000.

Allen, Ronald J., and Clark M. Williamson. *Preaching the Gospels without Blaming the Jews: A Lectionary Commentary.* Louisville: Westminster John Knox Press, 2004.

_____ . *Preaching the Old Testament: A Lectionary Commentary.* Louisville: Westminster John Knox Press, 2007.

Bartlett, David L. *Between the Bible and the Church: New Methods for Biblical Preaching.* Nashville: Abingdon Press, 1999.

Buttrick, David. *Homiletics: Moves and Structures.* Philadelphia: Fortress Press, 1987.

Craddock, Fred B. *As One without Authority: Revised and with New Sermons.* St. Louis: Chalice Press, 2001.

_____. *Preaching.* Nashville: Abingdon Press, 1985.

Forbes, James. *The Holy Spirit and Preaching.* Nashville: Abingdon Press, 1989.

Greenhaw, David M., and Ronald J. Allen, editors. *Preaching in the Context of Worship.* St. Louis: Chalice Press, 2000.

Hogan, Lucy Lind. *Graceful Speech: An Invitation to Preaching.* Louisville: Westminster John Knox Press, 2006.

Jeter, Joseph R., and Ronald J. Allen. *One Gospel, Many Ears: Preaching for Different Listeners in the Congregation.* St. Louis: Chalice Press, 2002.

Kay, James F. *Preaching and Theology.* St. Louis: Chalice Press, 2007.

Long, Thomas G. *Preaching and the Literary Forms of the Bible.* Philadelphia: Fortress Press, 1989.

_____. *The Witness of Preaching.* Second edition. Louisville: Westminster John Knox Press, 2005.

Lowry, Eugene L. *The Homiletical Plot: The Sermon as Narrative Art Form.* Revised edition. Louisville: Westminster John Knox Press, 2001.

_____. *The Sermon: Dancing the Edge of Mystery.* Nashville: Abingdon Press, 1997.

McClure, John S. *Preaching Words: 144 Key Terms in Homiletics.* Louisville: Westminster John Knox Press, 2007.

McClure, John S., Ronald J. Allen, Dale P. Andrews, L. Susan Bond, Dan P. Moseley, and G. Lee Ramsey Jr. *Listening to Listeners: Homiletical Case Studies.* St. Louis: Chalice Press, 2004.

McMickle, Marvin A. *Living Water for Thirsty Souls: Unleashing the Power of Exegetical Preaching.* Valley Forge, Pa.: Judson Press, 2001.

Mulligan, Mary Alice, Diane Turner-Sharazz, Dawn Ottoni Wilhelm, and Ronald J. Allen. *Believing in Preaching: What Listeners Hear in Sermons.* St. Louis: Chalice Press, 2005.

Pasquarello, Michael, III. *Christian Preaching: A Trinitarian Theology of Proclamation.* Grand Rapids: Baker Academic, 2006.

Proctor., Samuel D. *The Certain Sound of the Trumpet: Crafting a Sermon of Authority.* Valley Forge, Pa.: Judson Press, 1994.

Rice, Charles. *The Embodied Word: Preaching as Art and Liturgy.* Minneapolis: Augsburg Fortress, 1991.

Rose, Lucy Atkinson. *Sharing the Word: Preaching in the Roundtable Church.* Louisville: Westminster John Knox Press, 1997.

Sleeth, Ronald E. *God's Word and Our Words: Basic Homiletics.* Atlanta: John Knox Press, 1986.

Steimle, Edmund A., Morris J. Niedenthal, and Charles L. Rice. *Preaching the Story.* Philadelphia: Fortress Press, 1980.

Suchocki, Marjorie Hewitt. *The Whispered Word: A Theology of Preaching.* St. Louis: Chalice Press, 1999.

Thomas, Frank A. *They Like to Never Quit Praisin' God: The Role of Celebration in Preaching.* Cleveland: United Church Press, 1997.

Tisdale, Leonora Tubbs. *Preaching as Local Theology and Folk Art.* Minneapolis: Fortress Press, 1997.

Ward, Richard F. *Speaking of the Holy: The Art of Communication in Preaching.* St. Louis: Chalice Press, 2001.

Webb, Stephen H. *The Divine Voice: Christian Proclamation and the Theology of Sound.* Grand Rapids: Brazos Press, 2004.

Wilson, Paul Scott. *The Four Pages of the Sermon: A Guide to Biblical Preaching.* Nashville: Abingdon Press, 1999.

_____. *God Sense: Reading the Bible for Preaching.* Nashville: Abingdon Press, 2001.

Wisdom, Andrew Carl. *Preaching to a Multi-generational Assembly.* Collegeville, Minn.: Liturgical Press, 2004.

INDEX